This Is Not a Fighting Song

Short Theological Engagements with Popular Music

Series Editor: Christian Scharen

Editorial Committee: Margarita Simon Guillory, Jeff Keuss, Mary McDonough, Myles Werntz, Daniel White Hodge

Short Theological Engagements with Popular Music features theologians who have a passion for particular popular artists and who offer robust theological engagements with the work of that artist—engaging a song, an album, or a whole body of work over a career. Books in the series are accessible, yet deep both in their theological and musical engagement. Each book foregrounds ideas of interest in the musician's work, first, and puts these into conversation with the context and culture, second, and the Christian tradition, third. Each book, therefore, includes analysis of the cultural artifact, cultural context, and the relation to Christian tradition. Each book endeavors, as well, to speak with vitality to the challenges of living with God's mercy and justice in today's world.

This Is Not a Fighting Song

The Prophetic Witness of the
INDIGO GIRLS

Meredith Holladay

CASCADE *Books* · Eugene, Oregon

THIS IS NOT A FIGHTING SONG
The Prophetic Witness of the Indigo Girls

Short Theological Engagements with Popular Music

Cascade Books
An Imprint of Wipf and Stock Publishers
199 W. 8th Ave., Suite 3
Eugene, OR 97401

www.wipfandstock.com

PAPERBACK ISBN: 978-1-5326-0785-1
HARDCOVER ISBN: 978-1-5326-0787-5
EBOOK ISBN: 978-1-5326-0786-8

Cataloguing-in-Publication data:

Names: Holladay, Meredith, author.

Title: This is not a fighting song : the prophetic witness of the
    Indigo Girls / by Meredith Holladay.

Description: Eugene, OR: Cascade Books, 2022 | Series: Short
    Theological Engagements with Popular Music | Includes biblio-
    graphical references.

Identifiers: ISBN 978-1-5326-0785-1 (paperback) | ISBN 978-1-
    5326-0787-5 (hardcover) | ISBN 978-1-5326-0786-8 (ebook)

Subjects: LCSH: Indigo Girls (musical group) | Religion and cul-
    ture. | Popular music—Religious aspects.

Classification: ML3921.8.P67 H655 2022 (print) | ML3921.8.P67
    (ebook)

*To the Indigo Girls, of course, for your music, your words,
your work. It is all an inspiration.
For all my musical soul-mates along the way—the singalongs,
the concerts, this is all for you:
"The prize is always worth the rocky ride."
And, lastly, for Zach. Without you this would still be a dream.*

"My personal arc bends more towards hope and resurrection than complete despair."

— EMILY SALIERS

Contents

Acknowledgments

I discovered the Indigo Girls in high school, listening to a couple of upper classmen girls singing their songs for the talent show at our church youth camp. I couldn't tell you which song it was (it's been a few decades), but the song and the performance struck a chord with me. Perhaps at the time I just wanted to be cool like Thea and Vanessa, so I tried to be a fan, too. It wasn't until several years later, almost out of college, that I revisited that chord and the Girls and found playlist companions who would accompany me and help me sing my own songs (not literally; I'll leave that to Emily and Amy) from then on—from cassettes, to CDs, and playlists recorded onto both, to MP3s, iPods, and the cloud—the Indigo Girls have been a guiding light for me and so many others. This book would not be possible if it weren't for the deep and personal connection I feel with the music and lives of Amy Ray and Emily Saliers; and I know I am not alone.

As I wrote and revised these pages, I was struck repeatedly with gratitude for the friendships that have formed and deepened because of a shared love of the songs and albums of the Indigo Girls. My life would be much less vibrant without the friendships of fellow fans like Shannon Smythe, Becca Gillespie Messman, Sharyl Marshall

Dixon, Leah Grundset Davis, Stefanie Hayner Justice, Jenny McDevitt, Mandy Dunlap McNeely, and so many more who helped me sing along.

This book would never have found its way to completion without the quiet encouragement of my husband, Zach. He never nagged (even though I certainly could've used it), but accommodated my writing in weekend spurts, managing naptimes, mealtimes, bedtimes, and all kinds of other household things, and did so eagerly. Zach, your calm, steady presence and unwavering support is the reason these pages exist. Also, for Silas and Sawyer - you give me hope - may you never lose your imagination.

Lastly, with gratitude for everyone who supported this project along the way, be in nudges to keep writing, in excitement that kicked my hesitation back into effort, or in being one of my consistent conversation partners in the process. Thank you.

1

Introduction

The Indigo Girls

The Indigo Girls, the name given to the duo formed by Amy Ray and Emily Saliers, released their first recording in 1985, but the roots for their musical partnership stretch more than a decade prior. The two met in elementary school in Atlanta in 1974, as Amy recalls "across a lunch table in a cafeteria. I don't really remember much except the playground and the cafeteria scenes—girls gathered around Emily while she played her guitar."[1] Because Emily was a year ahead of Amy in school, the two did not become close friends until high school, when they were both in chorus together, which afforded them an opportunity for friendship and collaboration: "Being in the chorus

---

1. Ray, *A Year a Month*. All citations from Ray and Saliers, *A Year a Month* (blog) will be preceded by the writer of the particular blog entry being referenced. All quotes were retrieved on July 28, 2021; although, entries may no longer be available online due to the dynamic nature of blogs.

together truly bonded us, as it was a chance for kids from different grades to hang out, and Amy and I were immediately and deeply simpatico."[2] In 1981, while both still in high school, Amy and Emily began playing music together, and began playing as a "'cover song' bar band, both having fake i.d.'s and our parents' encouragement to carry on."[3] In the fall of 1981, Emily left for college at Tulane, and the following year, Amy began her freshman year at Vanderbilt. During the year they would visit each other and continue their musical partnership, fostered even deeper when home during breaks from school. In 1983, independent of each other, though fortuitous, they transferred to Emory University, landing them both back in Atlanta. This move provided obvious advantageous for their performance and partnership, as well as proved formative for their respective identities and activism that would characterize their career for several decades continuing into their current work.

Amy Ray grew up in a conservative home in Georgia; as she describes them, her family and home are quite typical for the South. She describes her family as "very conservative" and they "went to church about four days a week."[4] Though her family was conservative, and she wrestled with that as she got older and got more progressive, she reflects that her "parents were really cool and generous, very Southern . . . you worry about others before you worry about yourself . . . to the point that it's probably not a good thing!"[5] Amy contrasts her very entrenched, evangelical, Southern rearing with Emily's, noting that

2. Saliers, *A Year a Month.*
3. Saliers, *A Year a Month.*
4. Ray, "Persistence of Optimism."
5. Ray, "Persistence of Optimism."

"Emily grew up in a progressive family . . . [she was] raised knowing the importance of being engaged." Emily's family was an outlier because they were not rooted in the South: Emily is a Southern transplant; the Saliers family moved to Atlanta when she was eleven for her father's vocation. They moved from New Haven, Connecticut, where he had been teaching at Yale Divinity School. Don Saliers taught Worship and Sacred Music at Emory University's Candler School of Theology. Emily reflects on her family life as being progressive and open to asking questions, which gave her a foundation for her reflection and song writing.

The two women were barely out of college when they dubbed themselves the Indigo Girls and were touring, performing, and recording with the dedication and schedule of "true" professional musicians (in fact, Ray finished her senior year of college thanks to "the help of some cool Professors who let me do my work while on tour"[6]). They landed on the name somewhat randomly, searching the dictionary for words that sounded good, and landed on *Indigo,* which, according to Amy, resonated because it is "a significant Southern crop, fraught with the brutality of slavery, deadly working conditions, and international trade debacles . . . Subconsciously I might have been going for some subversion here, with such a dark underbelly to an innocent word."[7] Due in no small part to their determination and commitment to playing their music and having their music *played,* by 1988, they had landed a recording contract with Epic Records, and recorded their first full-length album, their self-titled debut, which was released in

6. Ray, *A Year a Month.*
7. Ray, *A Year a Month.*

3

March 1989, an album that went Gold within the year, and won the Best Contemporary Folk Album Grammy.[8]

The Indigo Girls continued songwriting, recording and releasing albums, and keeping up with a demanding publicity and tour schedule. As they continued to establish themselves in their career, they also established themselves as artist–activists, and as they both reflect, their activism continues to mean as much to them as any other piece of their decades-long career (and a topic discussed in much greater depth in the following pages). At the time of publication, The Indigo Girls have recorded 15 studio albums, three live albums, and two compilations. Amy Ray has released six solo records and owns her own label, Daemon Records (founded in 1990), and Emily Saliers has released one solo album, has co-written a book with her father, *A Song to Sing, a Life to Live: Reflections on Music as Spiritual Practice*, and has contributed to the Atlanta food scene as former co-owner of Watershed and founding investor of Flying Biscuit Café. Both Ray and Saliers maintain their homes in Georgia (and have for the duration of their career): Ray in rural Dahlonega, Georgia, and Saliers in the Atlanta suburb of Decatur.

Both Amy and Emily are openly queer (though, despite early rumors, they have never been in a romantic relationship with each other; they describe each other as easy and fast best friends). Their songwriting and activism as they relate to LGBTQ+ issues and their own queerness

8. They were also nominated for Best New Artist that same year; the award would go to the disgraced duo Milli Vanilli. Perhaps it is a good thing they did not win the Best New Artist category, as many have seen this category as "cursed," translating to winners' careers quickly fading after winning. For example, past winners include: Starlight Vocal Band, Men at Work, LeAnn Rimes, and Evanescence (c.f. https://www.buzzfeed.com/moniquemelendez/the-best-new-artist-curse).

will be discussed at length in a later chapter. As it relates to their identities as musicians and how their sexuality affected their career, the topic does bear mentioning in conjunction with some discussion about their coming out.

The Indigo Girls reflect on their coming out in contrasting tones: the private coming out—to themselves, each other, to those close to them—and the more public coming out, specifically as it related to their burgeoning popularity and hopes for success in their music career. Coming of age both as young adults and as musicians in the South, in the eighties, they had to deal with layers of stigma surrounding their gender presentations and queerness. On the one hand, each reflects on her coming out as almost a nonissue. Emily remembers it this way: "I had a fear of coming out . . . I thought we'd get stigmatized, which we did. In the end it *so* didn't matter at all."[9] Yet, a closer listen reveals latent, lingering struggle. Amy reflects that she wrestled for *years* with the internal struggle, not fully understanding who she was: "I went through years of self-hate, I was a cutter, I had a lot of problems . . . I didn't try to *not* be gay, but I had an internalized homophobia, even though I had a girlfriend."[10] She refers to her own homophobia as *internalized* consistently. Despite being one of three gay sisters in her family, Amy acknowledges that her family's Southern, conservative roots meant they "struggled hard with coming out and acceptance."[11] Whereas Emily's struggle seemed to be more on the public level, Amy's stemmed from her more conservative family and upbringing, leaving her little room to understand herself outside of the fixed notions of acceptability in evangelical Georgia.

9. Tongson, "Emily Saliers."
10. Tongson, "Amy Ray."
11. Ray, "A Year a Month."

Conversely, Emily relates little of the struggle on the personal level—though it was Amy who came out first—if measuring such things tells us anything at all. Emily relates that she was briefly, and personally fearful of homosexuality: "just before I started to discover that I thought I might be gay, I was very homophobic. I remember thinking, 'ugh, homosexuality, that's perverse; I don't know anybody who does that . . . ' I didn't know what it was so I didn't know how to react." However, as she describes her own coming out, once she "realized" she was gay, she never really had any internal struggle with it: "I never felt bad about it; I never felt like this is wrong or I'm going to fight this, I just realized what it was, finally."[12] She relates that her family (perhaps to the surprise of many interviewers, considering her father is a Methodist minister, and she grew up going to church), has always been completely supportive. Saliers has also been asked if her Christian background and spirituality has caused her conflict with her sexuality, to which she responds:

> I have never had a spiritual struggle with being gay. I think those that do suffer from years and years of spiritual misinterpretation, and that God created us to love each other. When two people love each other consensually and with respect, it doesn't matter if they are of the same sex. In time, the evolution of gay rights . . . will make us look back and wonder why there was such hatred and homophobia.[13]

She repeated this sentiment in an interview with the *Huffington Post*: "It's a schizophrenic feeling to be involved in church life and then feel that there are so many people that

12. Wolf et al., "INDIGO GIRLS."
13. Saliers, "Emily's Answers."

stand against you. Personally, I've never had an issue with my sexuality and my faith. I felt like I was born to be who I am and I never had issues."[14]

By both accounts, the Saliers family has always been progressive—though certainly not too difficult a label to earn in evangelical Atlanta circles. In more recent conversations about their coming out, their geographic context perhaps makes it difficult to understand their story contrasted with today's more inclusive culture. Amy also offers a reflection, revealing how much the context and cultural language around sexuality and coming how has evolved: "We didn't know when we were in high school what the word *gay* meant. We thought gay was bestiality. We were sheltered to the point of crazy."[15] In a 2021 interview, she reflects on how, even as a woman in her fifties, current LGBTQ+ movements have helped her understand herself in ways that she did not have the vocabulary for when she was younger, which caused her a lot of angst and despair: "I was a cutter sometimes. I was just going through this real struggle with my body and my sexuality and everything . . . There's this male in me that is so at odds with this female part of my body," a conflict she was ill-equipped to process some 30–40 years ago: "I didn't know there was such a fluidity." The trans-rights movement has helped her understand that, "I ID as genderqueer . . . [and] my pronoun is *she;* that's what I embrace."[16]

As both Amy and Emily were understanding their queerness on a personal level, they were grappling with the implications in the music industry (corporate labels, commercial radio, music management, etc.) of being two

14. Moss, "Emily Saliers."

15. Ray, "Persistence of Optimism."

16. Masters, "Amy Ray."

lesbians from the South. Almost immediately, they pushed back against the music industry's attempts to pigeonhole them as a "gay band." Before they encountered homophobia at the industry level, they were struck by how pervasive homophobia is within the entire music system. In a blog post, Amy looks back on those early years and realizes, "We weren't totally acquainted with the ways in which our sexuality played into the 'outsider' status of the Alt music world, but I can remember feeling a little shunned in the 'coffee house' world, which at the time was actually pretty traditional and straight."[17] Their career—from playing as a bar band, to emerging as professional musicians under a major label—all took place at a time when women were not equal as artists, and being queer was far from commonplace—as an identity and in terms of acceptance. Sexism layered with homophobia presented hurdles and roadblocks along their journey. Being gay in the eighties and early nineties was almost always accompanied by the stigma surrounding HIV/AIDS—an oft-misunderstood disease that brought with it fear and ostracization. Amy relates that she came to terms with the reality of their image as a "lesbian folk duo" before Emily did. Emily wrestled much more with the inevitable (in many ways, already present) "pigeonhole," so much so that, while out to friends and family, she had not yet publicly self-identified as lesbian in her role as part of the Indigo Girls. Both joke about the poorly kept secret, but Amy maintains she wanted to respect Emily's timing. They recall an interview around 1991–1992, at a college radio press conference. In response to a question, Emily came out rather nonchalantly as part of her answer.

17. Ray, *A Year a Month*.

Amy reflects on her perspective at the time: "I get that we don't want to be pigeonholed as this lesbian folk duo, but we already are. Either way you're crucified; let's just be out. We're asking everyone in the audience to be individuals and believe in themselves . . . but we're not willing to be who we are." She gives a lot of credit to their loyal audience for helping her get over her hesitation and embrace who they are: "Being openly gay *did* alienate people because everything was so conservative and backwards. We were just suffering under fear. It was fear . . . [but] it's like an agreement with our audience. We're asking everyone to be themselves and we gotta do the same thing."[18] Emily echoes this conviction, as she discusses coming to terms with her sexuality publicly: "Once it became so clear that I was gay and I had a great life and we had a lot of support . . . do not turn away from the lesbians who supported you when there were two people in the room. . . . You're saying there's something that's not valid about the people who supported you from the very beginning."[19] Both agree that their audience, growing both in number and in loyalty, prompted and emboldened them to embrace their queerness, both publicly as individuals and as part of the identity of their band. As they look back on those early days, they both recognize and give credit to the ways their audience helped them understand, accept, and grow into their queerness, and encouraged them to embrace fully who they are—pigeonhole be damned!

Throughout their career they have established themselves as a progressive voice—not just among folk musicians—taking seriously what they see as their responsibility to advocate for others, seek justice, and speak truth

18. Masters, "Amy Ray."
19. Tongson, "Emily Saliers."

9

to power. The following chapters, by way of an in-depth examination of their discography, will explore themes that connect them to the (Christian) prophetic tradition, and examine ways that their music breaks down lines between what is secular and sacred, thereby offering a voice of theological reflection through their music, lyrics, and activist justice work.

2

Defining the Terms

Creativity: The Image of God

This project will focus specifically on music as a powerful form of enjoying God in this artistic sense. Music is one way we express, interpret, and understand the world around us. In this way, the creative sense within us can and must be taken seriously as a theological endeavor and as theological epistemology. Art can serve as a means of knowledge and understanding; therefore music is also religiously and theologically significant.[1]

The Psalmist proclaims God's creation by singing of the beauty of God: "Make a joyful noise to God, all the earth; sing the glory of God's name; give to God glorious

1. I use the terms "religious" and "theological" throughout this project as related but distinct approaches. "Theological" assumes a specific starting point, and specific set of questions about what it means to be human in relation to a sacred. "Religious," on the other hand, refers to the more sociological reference points that analyze religion on substantive and functional terms.

praise."[2] This book builds on the assumption that creativity, creative action, and artistic endeavors are ordained, blessed by God: "the artist is the creator like God creates."[3] Because God created us, and we are created in the image of God, we are, then, created to create: "making beautiful forms is theologically connected to our call both to listen and respond to God in prayer, praise, and sacrament."[4] Therefore, the artistic inclination and ability in all of us, whether to create or to enjoy creativity and appreciate others' creations, are not merely a *part* of being human; they can also be a means of understanding God and who we are as God's creation. Coud it be they are the very spirit and soul of *how* God created us to be?

Dorothy Sayers bases her contribution to theological aesthetics and literary theory on a similar claim. She states, "The characteristic common to God and man is apparently that: the desire and the ability to make things."[5] Artistry and creativity allow us to be fully human: these creative endeavors serve as reflection of our image of God shared by both men and women, but they are also a means to enjoy God and understand God. It is not just in the creation or act of artistry, but in the appreciation of these efforts of others. The spirit of creativity could be likened to the movement of the Holy Spirit.[6] It is that which brings to life the world around us—recognizing the beauty of creation in sights, sounds, touch, smell—and stemming from that life it provides the inspiration to participate, to make and enjoy our own sights, sounds, smells, textures.

2. Ps 66:1 NRSV.

3. Wolterstorff, *Art in Action*, 52.

4. Dyrness, *Visual Faith*, 9.

5. Sayers, *Mind of the Maker*, 22.

6. Moltmann, *Spirit of Life*.

Others, like Sayers, have elaborated on the artistic endeavors as means to enjoy God, to understand God, thereby as means by which we are more fully human—living out our God-ordained existence. This informs and demonstrates that the arena for arts, artistry, and creativity spans wider and deeper than the traditional "fine arts"—what we often think of as belonging in museums or concert halls. Likewise, the democratization of culture and technology (developments some attribute to globalization), as well as the spread of mass media, contribute to the accessibility of the worlds of creativity.[7] The widespread impact and manifold forms of cultural products demonstrates that artistic endeavors and products have something to tell us about our world, the people in it, and how we relate to and understand God. This has led to a burgeoning path of religious scholars who look to popular culture as significant, a path to which this project aims to contribute.

Oliver Sacks, in *Musicophilia,* addresses the unique power of music in human life and experience. Interested in the scientific and medical connections between the brain and music, Sacks insists that there is something about music that resonates with the cognitive and neurological function of being human. He further argues for the integration of music with both the intellectual and the emotional facets of human experience: "Yet music calls to both parts of our nature—it is essentially emotional, as it is essentially intellectual. Often when we listen to music, we

7. Some would denigrate this development, arguing that the democratization and spread of mass media has contributed to the erosion of quality art. This, and other theories of culture, will be explored further in the following chapter, further articulating this mourning of the loss of "genuine" art, or the ability to recognize "good," "quality," or "true" art.

are conscious of both: we may be moved to the depths even as we appreciate the formal structure of composition."[8]

However, the communal aspect of music must not be dismissed or overlooked, and is particularly germane to conversations about the Indigo Girls. Music festivals, concerts, Facebook groups and other social networking venues, and music writing all demonstrate the power of music to unite people through shared experiences. Jeanette Bicknell further asserts this point, that music is first and fundamentally social. She states that music cannot be experienced alone: "The fact that music can have a private or individual use does not make it any less a social product. We are creatures of society; the fact that we sometimes want a break from other people . . . does not make us any less so. Communing with music is a form of communing with human reality, and that is social."[9]

Music can be a source of revelation—a source of theological reflection on the divine, the world, and our place among and in relation to them. This is no less true for music (and culture in general) outside any "official" religious tradition. Some may draw a bright line and call this music "secular;" however, both Emily and Amy (of the Indigo Girls) intentionally blur the lines between "sacred" and "secular" music, in order to recognize the powerful potential for theological reflection in the perhaps unexpected sources of popular music.

Before going much further, it would be prudent to pause and define what is meant by theological reflection. Discussing theology includes asking existential questions and considering broad themes of what it means to be human (individual existence), how we are one among many

8. Sacks, *Musicophilia*, 312.

9. Bicknell, *Why Music Moves Us*, 93.

(society), and how we understand God in relation to these questions (the transcendent, the sacred). From this comes the themes of identity, loss, hope, evil, suffering, redemption, and justice. Popular music can, thus, be a starting point for theology. In order to take these voices seriously as theologians, we must also have in view an idea of theology as something that can and does take place in the realm of the "popular." That is, we are all theologians, and theology happens when we ask questions about grace, suffering, sin, and redemption. I use the phrase "prophetic witness" to further clarify and name what I intend by exploring the theological reflection of music.

Walter Brueggeman defines the prophetic task "to nurture, nourish, and evoke a consciousness and perception alternative to the consciousness and perception of the dominant culture around us."[10] Prophets do not just announce; they call to action and transformation, thus empowering people to engage in history. Brueggeman offers a further definition of the prophetic ministry, which "consists of offering an alternative perception of reality and in letting people see their own history in the light of God's freedom and [God's] will for justice. . . . The prophetic imagination can be discerned wherever people try to live together and show concern for their shared future and identity."[11] Therefore, the prophetic witness of music to the experience of being humans, as well as often being overt forms of protest, will also prove significant manifestations of music's power and potential to offer an alternative perception of reality.

These issues will direct our attention to the general concept of a prophetic voice or witness in society. I will

10. Brueggemann, *Prophetic Imagination*, 3.

11. Brueggemann, *Prophetic Imagination*, 116–17.

argue that not only can we locate streams of prophetic witness throughout human history, but we *must* find strains of this tradition of prophetic witness among us. It is a specific theological claim, and one that is central to this project: the prophetic spirit bears witness to the providence, care, and ongoing creation of God in the world. We believe God cares about the world, and we believe part of the human task of co-creating is providing and caring for the world, including the ongoing nurturing of human solidarity and community. The prophetic witness speaks out to and is in service of these creative tasks.

Music again—outside the walls of the church—contains potential for theological reflection, and in its unique capacity to resonate among humanity, it serves as a prophetic witness for those both within and outside the church walls. While these are explicitly theological claims about culture and popular music, it would be irresponsible to project a clear theological intent on the part of the songwriters as a necessary condition for the presence of this prophetic witness. To be sure, authorial intent is important, but, for the purposes of identifying theological reflection and prophetic spirit, these effectual elements—the audience reception and interpretation—may be even more important.

In order to demonstrate these more abstract concepts of theological reflection and prophetic witness, I will focus on both the Indigo Girls' music and their audience. The following chapters will engage with the music of the artists, identifying themes such as pain, suffering, hope, and redemption. Many of these themes relate to what it means to be human manifest in issues of relationship—to others and to the divine. In addition to specific reading of the "texts," the music and lyrics of these artists, attention must be paid to the artists themselves. One of the most intriguing themes in their work is the political: the element of protest present both in the music itself but also in the activism of the artists. The prophetic witness and imagination manifest in this unique ability of musicians to combine deeply personal expressions and explorations of themes of humanity, suffering, and redemption, and the impetus toward protest, engaging with the larger community and social systems.

What is Theology?

Theological reflection deals with broad questions of human life, relationships to others and to God, thus ranging from the individual, to the collective, to the transcendent and sacred. From that come the themes of identity, loss, hope, evil, suffering, redemption, and justice. In order to take seriously voices in culture and art as theologians, we must also have in view an idea of theology as something that can and does take place in the realm of the "popular," in the true sense of the word—"of the people"—i.e., we are all theologians, and theology happens when we are seeking answers to questions about grace, suffering, sin, and redemption.

Most definitions of theology begin by examining its etymology. Theology comes from the Greek *theo* and *logos:* words about God, discourse about God, ideas about God. According to Karen Armstrong, Aristotle believed theology "was the 'first philosophy' because it was concerned with the highest mode of being."[12] This philosophical theology remained simply that—an intellectual exercise in abstraction. An abstract theology is really no theology at

12. Armstrong, *Case for God*, 72.

all; insofar as it emerges from a specific tradition, and as soon as it describes a specific understanding of the divine, theology is specific. William Dyrness defines theological reflection as "simply the practice of naming and describing the major commitments that guide thought and action."[13] His definition would square with Paul Tillich who defines religion as "the substance, the ground and the depth of man's [sic] spiritual life . . . his *ultimate concern*."[14] *Theology, therefore, must be personal and specific.*

According to Daniel Migliore, Christian theology is concerned with "the understanding of God as triune, the centrality of Jesus Christ and his work of reconciliation, and the hope of fulfillment of life in communion with God and with all others by the power of the Holy Spirit."[15] While the two former primary concerns are certainly important, some may even argue foundational, they are not often explicitly in the cultural forms addressed in the following chapters. Though it may at times be appropriate to overlap these concerns with the message and/or interpretation of pieces of music, the ways music (and lyrics) wrestle with hope and the necessity of life in communion with God and others, (or, by contrast the struggle when this fulfillment seems out of reach) will be much more obvious. *Theology, therefore, is a reflection on hope and reconciliation, in response to specific contexts.*

Paul Tillich champions cultural forms as valid and vital means of expressing these ultimate concerns: "Pictures, poems, and music can become objects of theology, not from the point of view of their aesthetic form, but from the point of view of their power of expressing some aspects

13. Dyrness, *Visual Faith*, 87.
14. Tillich, *Dynamics of Faith*, xvii.
15. Migliore, *Faith Seeking Understanding*, xi.

of that which concerns us ultimately, in and through their aesthetic form."[16] Here the unique ability of art (visual, music, language) stands out as able to stand in this correlative "middle ground." As Tillich articulates, aesthetic forms have the unmatched capacity to connect to and express the depths of human experience—persons' deepest hopes, fears, despair, faith, and love (and the lack of any or all of these). The expressive capability of artistic forms ought to be instructive for those doing theology, in bringing to light the objects of "ultimate concern," to which theology must find an answer if it is to speak a Christian message. David Tracy revises Tillich's approach: instead of responding from a tradition to questions posed by "external" cultural forces, Tracy calls us not only to listen to the existential questions that arise from position of aesthetic forms, but also appeals to openness in finding *answers* implied in such cultural forms.[17]

According to Dorothee Sölle, "the object of theology can only be the relationship between God and human beings: in other words, reflection on the experiences that have compelled human beings to talk about something like 'God.'"[18] Therefore, theological reflection includes wrestling with ideas of creation, sin, grace, resurrection (redemption), and the church. *In sum, theology is specific, grounded in particular contexts, dealing with individual and collective human experiences.*

On a slightly different place along the spectrum, several writers who focus their study on theology, religion, and culture identify theology with an eye toward cultural conversation. Jeremy Begbie, who focuses primarily on

16. Tillich, *Systematic Theology*, 13.

17. Tracy, *Analogical Imagination*.

18. Sölle, *Thinking about God*, 1.

music, claims all Christians are theologians. Because of this claim, we should avoid limiting theological conversations to what seem like the "official" church or "official" dogma, or anything that requires some sort of authoritative seal of approval; his perspective is thoroughly egalitarian and democratic. He defines theology as "the disciplined thinking and rethinking of the Christian gospel for the sake of fostering a wisdom that is nourished by, and nourishes, the church in its worship and mission of the world."[19] Elaine Graham further illustrates the connection between theological reflection and cultural studies. When we study culture, we are studying the ways that people create meaning—both for themselves as individuals, and collectively. In that same way, she calls theology a practice; just as other cultural practices are meaning-making, theology is "one of the activities by which human beings build worlds of meaning and significance, and experience themselves as creative, moral, and purposeful beings."[20] *Theology, therefore, is an activity available to all persons, through which we create and discover meaning.*

If theology emerges from particular contexts and speaks to lived experiences, then theological reflection must include narrative in both its form and quality. Attention to human stories resounds with the lived nature of theology; the telling, hearing, and sharing of stories are theological acts. Because theology begins within and reflects upon lived, human experience, and because it tells a story, then a significant facet of its function for individuals and communities is reflection on what it means to be human. Theology interprets human experience; through the telling of stories and the reflection on praxis, theology

19. Begbie, *Resounding Truth*, 19.
20. Graham, "What We Make of the World," 66.

addresses the reality and totality of human life, acknowledging and interpreting experiences of love, hope, fear, despair, pain, healing, suffering, and reconciliation. The significance of emphasizing the totality of human experience addresses the inadequacies of limited language and the impossibility of dividing human experience between "religious" and "everything else," an impossibility, the attempt at which often results in inauthenticity.

In anticipating the critique that cultural relevancy is equated to relativism, these theologies carry an implicit and thorough "no," instead insisting that theology *begins* with cultural relevancy. The solution (if there is one, it is surely not exhaustive) seems to be fuller attention to the sum of human experience—from birth to death, from elation to despair, from seen to unseen. McClendon remarks upon the importance of taking into account *all* of what it means to be human—the beauty *and* the pain: "unless theology can hear her own witnesses, unless she can take death in deadly earnest, take its grim enmity into her counsels and be shaped thereby, she ceases to be a serious discipline . . . Theology must hear her witnesses, discover her own truth, shape her doctrine in faithfulness to that truth."[21]

To question the presence, concern, or ability of God in the affairs of the world is not to deny faith; doubt is not heretical. Rather, as Geoffrey Wainwright says, this questioning, this darkness "implies relationship," which leads to the conclusion that this attitude of absence is an integral experience of the life of faith, and to deny it or ignore it is a disingenuous engagement in human existence in relationship to God.[22] This, I find, reflects the human tendency toward despair—the posture of hands in the air barely even

21. McClendon, *Biography as Theology*, 107.
22. Wainwright, *Doxology*, 42.

able to mutter a pitiful "why me?" The image of wrestling is instructive, which likely calls to mind the story of Jacob wrestling with God (or the angel of God) on the shores of the Jabbok. Jacob struggled with the deity, and out of that experience left forever changed—he bore a physical limp and a new name, Israel, the chosen of God.[23] This human wrestling is also the wrestling of our own experience and our own confusion at the unanswerables of life. We wrestle with expectations, broken hearts, unsatisfactory relationships, and empty pursuits. Wainwright aligns even these struggles as struggles with God, because we are struggling with our own purpose and our own identity, with the end goal (at least in the life of faith) of fulfilling God's design for the world, for society, and for ourselves.[24]

The church, meant in the most general sense, responds to the needs of the people—*all people*. Theology as a second step means that it is not limited to those who have degrees or those who have special knowledge, insight, or ordination. Rather, theological language observes, participates in, and absorbs the experiences of the world—of hope, despair, love, hatred, anxiety, confusion, and community—and reflects on those things through the lens of faith. Christian theology addresses these human concerns, primarily in the nature, form, and substance of hope. Jürgen Moltmann, considering the all to human dissatisfaction and restlessness with the way the world is, notes, "peace with God means conflict with the world, for the goad of the promised future stabs inexorably into the flesh of every unfulfilled present."[25] However, we are not satisfied with passive acceptance of "the way things are."

---

23. Gen 32:22–31.

24. Wainwright, *Doxology*, 42–44.

25. Moltmann, *Theology of Hope*, 21.

According to Moltmann, the primary purpose of Christianity is in its vision of hope, and the nature of this hope is imaginative. Hope imagines an alternate future, a restored state of affairs, but this imagining reflects on the present by "revolutionizing and transforming the present."[26]

It is this imaginative quality that connects the theological to the creative. I noted previously that the *imago dei* spoken into existence in the second chapter of Genesis has been interpreted many ways, not least of which is indentifying the image of God as the creative and imaginative nature of humans; we are creative and imaginative creatures with the capacity to tell stories, create art, and dream of things as being other than they are. This imagination is also for many the core of Christian hope. Not only does hope imagine alternate states of affairs, but through the power of hope we are able to bring about these alternatives. Through our capacity for and calling toward hope we create the world the way we envision it to be—the way it *could* and *ought* to be.

As observed above, the link between creativity, imagination, and hope is more than coincidental. The value of creativity can be applied here in its ability to help us see other ways of human relationship and social structures; the creative impulse allows us to see how things *could be*. These theological qualities and themes show up quite notably in popular music. Because lyrics speak out of human experiences and tell stories, and music's unique ability to allow both performers and audiences to transcend their mundane experiences through the confluence of melody, harmony, rhythm, dissonance, combined with the lyrics, music is able to communicate theological themes in ways that resonate deeper than words alone might allow. In so

26. Moltmann, *Theology of Hope,* 16.

far as music denounces systems, political oppression, or inequality, and proclaims that this is not how we *ought* to live, and/or proclaims an alternative world, it speaks in concert with the qualities and nature of hope. The long-standing tradition of protest music is instructive on this point.

Of course, the flip-side of these proclamations is the tendency toward despair. Certainly music speaks out of this human location, and perhaps these examples will be far easier to identify. Because theology must emerge from and speak authentically to the full reality of human life, music that reflects doubt, pain, suffering, and despair is as important as that which proclaims hope, love, and redemption. In fact, as is the focus of the following three chapters, most popular music sings from the middle ground, expressing doubt, and seeking hope, but rarely falling into either situation with much ease.

3

The Sacred in the Everyday

Spirituality, Theology, and the Indigo Girls

Emily co-wrote, with her father, *A Song to Sing, A Life to Live: Reflections on Music as Spiritual Practice*, a book in Jossey-Bass's *The Practices of Faith* Series. In it, she writes: "Music and faith are, for me, intimately related, even as I continue to wrestle with questions about organized religion."[1] She sees "music . . . [as] some kind of mysterious mediator between us and the God we seek."[2] Part of the goal of writing this book together—a professor of sacred music and ordained minister, and his lesbian, folk-rock songwriter daughter—is to break down the typical sacred-secular boundaries between "Saturday night" and "Sunday morning" music. Both Don and Emily argue that these categories are useless, because the creators and the listeners to music remain the same people regardless of externally-pronounced transcendent (or not) quality: "the point is to notice that we are in the presence of a human

1. Saliers and Saliers, *Song to Sing*, 4.
2. Saliers and Saliers, *Song to Sing*, 5.

soul and to listen with care and respect from the depths of our own souls."[3] Much of the Indigo Girls' music is wrapped up in these definitions of music and its power. Though both Emily and Amy are hesitant to align with any particular religious dogma, religious themes persist throughout their songs. The following reflection from *A Song to Sing* is instructive in how we can understand their music as religious, even though by institutional accounts many would consider it "secular":

> Music can evoke the divine and not necessarily mention God all the time. Not all music with religious import needs to be explicitly liturgical . . . [or] addressed to God . . . At the same time, any music that explores human life in all its range of extremity and ordinariness can evoke the presence (or absence) of God. Music that moves toward the good, the true, the just, and the beautiful often brings a sense of transcendence to hearers . . . Some nonchurch music that truly expresses the heart's torment, the soul's lament, or the ecstatic joy we experience within the beauty of creation may be more religious than hymns with poor theology sung without conviction.[4]

As the Indigo Girls' career has extended into three decades, and as Emily has matured, she notes that she's "not afraid of religion anymore."[5] While many of their earlier songs dance around some of these more spiritual themes—often fraught with temptation toward despair —their later songs more frequently bend toward hope. For her part, Emily believes that "it's people who screw up

3. Saliers and Saliers, *Song to Sing*, 16.

4. Saliers and Saliers, *Song to Sing*, 165.

5. Saliers and Saliers, "Creativity Conversation.".

God's true message. Can't blame it on God; can't blame it on Jesus; can't blame it on Buddha . . . All the major faith figures have wanted nothing but for people to love each other, and we just get in our own ways."[6]

Writing the book with her father was a transformative experience for Emily, in that it challenged her to name, claim, and embrace her own religion and spirituality in ways that she previously felt no small amount of tension: "I had always kept my faith private, even though my spiritual experience growing up was one of openness and questioning, certainly not dogmatic or oppressive or judgmental." The focus of the book is of course on music, and how it is "undeniably central in our human search for meaning and belonging and getting in touch with mysteries,"[7] themes developed and explored in the following sections.

The first set of Indigo Girls songs will be discussed with this perspective in mind, looking at examples of songs that could be considered religious: some explicitly use religious language; others are more vague; all of them are significant insofar as they explore the fullness of human experience, opening "us to what is most real in humanity's suffering and glory, and in the mystery of the God who is searching for us, a source of life and hope deeper than we can conceive."[8]

One of their earliest songs, "hey jesus," takes the shape of a conversation, or a prayer, to Jesus. The singer allows that she does not often communicate with Jesus; and the song continues with a confession of sorts, followed by a supplication: "I am not your faithful servant, I hang around sometimes with a bunch of your black sheep, but

6. Saliers and Saliers, "Creativity Conversation."
7. Saliers, *A Year a Month.*
8. Saliers and Saliers, *Song to Sing*, 181.

if you make my baby stay, I'll make it up to you and that's a promise I will keep."[9] This particular song is an excerpt in what appears to be a string of conversations she has attempted with who she feels is a divine intercessor, however estranged she may be. The substance of the song shifts from her relationship and heartbreak to deeper theological questions. She compares her own lonely existence to Jesus: "it's easy for you, you got friends all over the world, you had the whole world waiting for your birth but now I ain't got nobody, I don't know what my life's worth."

Here the singer risks complete honesty, fueled by a position of utter despair. She clearly feels abandoned—both by her "baby" and by Jesus. She begins by asking Jesus to bring her lover back, but the song falls into a place of desperation, questioning Jesus on where he is and how he chooses to use his power. According to this song, Jesus is all-powerful and utterly transcendent; although she addresses him directly and rather intimately, there is a sense that she lacks any response or sense of presence that would convince her otherwise that Jesus cares about her situation. She feels her time and words are in vain, particularly in the closing line of the song in which she asks why she must wait until after this life to get concrete answers to her questions. Through the words of this prayer, out of her desperation, she also longs to identify with Jesus, or perhaps implore him to identify with her plight, saying that the whole world is waiting for him to come, and now she

9. A note about the quoted lyrics throughout: Where the lyrics have been quoted directly from the Indigo Girls' website (indigorgirls. com/discographyandlyrics; no longer online), accessed throughout 2009 and 2010, I have left them as originally published online. Some of their lyrics are given in verse form with line-breaks and clear punctuation. Others (such as "hey jesus") are given sans capitalization and punctuation. Lyrics that are not recalled directly from their website, I have chosen to use more traditional verse line breaks.

is waiting for him, once more, to come and fix her situation. Instead, she seems to beg of him, desperate, for some sign or clue that he will intercede. This song represents the depths of doubt and despair that are common to the human experience. From the Indigo Girls' first full-length album, *Strange Fire*, "hey jesus" also comes at the naissance of their career, when both singers were young. This is significant because it communicates the position of late-adolescence/early-adulthood in which most things of life are unknowns, and the future feels heavy.[10] That, coupled with spiritual seeking and darkness, are powerful because they are universal to the human experience and human development.

Another song that speaks to physical and spiritual despair is "Prince of Darkness," from their second and self-titled full-length album. Emily reflected on this song's theme, which is about:

> my own constant battle with my inner darkness, and the prince of darkness [is], obviously, the diabolical force. So it's about light and darkness. And how darkness, you can feel sometimes like it almost is going to pull you under. But there are people in your life who can save you . . . And it's like, in the end, it's an affirmative statement. I'm not going to be a pawn for the prince of darkness. You know, I have the strength to find my light rather than to dwell in my darkness.[11]

The song begins by setting up a contrast: "My place is of the sun and this place is of the dark," and continues as the singer reflects on the world around her. The images we are given reflect on the desperation she sees around her.

---

10. The dark night of the soul, perhaps.
11. Wiser, "Emily Saliers."

She is haunted by these images, as she compares them to bad dreams. The images that follow are haunting indeed: "And now someone's on the telephone, desperate in his pain / Someone's on the bathroom floor doing her cocaine / . . . / No one can convince me we aren't gluttons for our doom." These images are gritty, and reflect lives lacking hope, those who have given in to pain, desperation, even suicide. The people described here, however, are to be understood as *others*; there is an intentional distance between the hopelessness of those described and the singer. She sets her own life up as a contrast, a contrast that is not merely existential or situational—between sadness and happiness, or happenstance. Rather, the difference she sees between these others who seem buried in their own desperation and pain and herself rests on a spiritual level; it is vague. She uses words like "Providence," and sets up a light/dark contrast, so we hear her struggle. The powerful language that follows testifies to her capacity to feel others' pain and her desire to find a salve and offers a raw glimpse at the struggle of living in the world where "we are gluttons for our doom," meaning where we are constantly battered by temptations toward despair and pain. With the words, "My heart beat like the wings of wild birds in a cage," she hints at a longing for freedom from these temptations.

The hints we get as to how Emily resists the burdens of the world come in these lines: "(By grace, my sight grows stronger and I will not / be a pawn for the Prince of Darkness any longer) / My greatest hope my greatest cause to grieve." She attributes the power of grace to be able to see more clearly in order to resist the power of darkness, here using one of the proper names traditionally associated with Satan. The last line here is curious: from the same source come both deep hope and grief. If her hope is found in the antithesis of the Prince of Darkness, and in Providence, then we can interpret this to be a spiritual sense of hope in opposition to darkness, grief, and despair. Perhaps this serves as both a source of grace and grief because she is able to see all the people who *have* given over to the darkness.

The tension between despair and hope emerges throughout the Indigo Girls' canon, often relying on the contrast between light and darkness. Other examples of lyrics to this effect include the song "123," off their 1990 release *Nomads Indians Saints:* "How long can you be agile, dancing between the alter [sic] and the mercy seat? / Here's a chance to make a choice, are you aware of the fire beneath your feet?" And from the same album, "Hand Me Downs:" " . . . all with hope that / Emptiness brings fullness and / Loss of love brings wholeness to us all." These contrasts often illustrate a dance between two worlds, demonstrating the mixture of sacred and secular that is intrinsic to living as a spiritual being yet embodied on the earth and in relation to other human beings, and attempting to understand or relate to God, variously understood. This tension—or blending, really—is not accidental; Emily reflects that she believes she "became a better writer when [she] accepted the ugliness of life." Once she learned to "express even the most shocking things," she discovered that she could and would break down barriers—beginning with her own internal barriers.[12]

Throughout the Indigo Girls' catalog, religious language also persists in songs about love relationships, offering images and interpretations of what "real love" is, and through words about living in general that parallel language of spirituality and spiritual journey. The themes are

12. Saliers and Saliers, "Creativity Conversation."

wrapped in a search for greater, deeper meaning to life, the question underlying *what is a life well-lived?* Many of these examples rest on the assumption that relationships involve dependency, and our personal identity, and even spiritual well-being is wrapped up in our relationships with other people—our willingness to open up to others and to allow others into our own lives. As they talk about love, language of gift is often present. For example, the song "Love's Recovery," from their 1989 *Indigo Girls* album, looks back on a time when "it was hard to turn the other cheek." The singer reflects on that past and clearly feels she is in a different place, mentally and spiritually. As she looks around and reflects on the past, she realizes the naïveté of believing that love conquers all. Rather, that love can persist, or does persist, she feels, is "slim chance." She uses theological language as she goes on to reflect:

> Oh how I wish I were a trinity, so if I lost a part of me
> I'd still have two of the same to live
> But nobody gets a lifetime rehearsal, as specks of dust
>   we're universal
> To let this love survive would be the greatest gift we
>   could give . . .
> Though it's storming out I feel safe within the
>   arms of love's recovery.

This desire, expressed in the paradoxical Christian Trinitarian form is not so much for divine power, but because she believes she would not feel so alone facing the heartbreak that feels like she has lost part of her own identity; the heartbreak that is at once as mundane as breathing, and as unique and deeply personal as a fingerprint. The symbol here thereby reflects the relational interpretations of the Christian Triune God. She follows those lines with a recognition of her own human finitude, calling on the image of ashes and dust from the Old Testament: ". . . until you return to the ground for out of it you were taken; you are dust, and to dust you shall return."[13] What does give her solace in the end is that love has survived (or "recovered") and that is what she has, and all she needs to keep her feeling safe; she closes these thoughts with her own love, realized as a gift.

Other songs in their catalog relate to love and relationship as part of a struggle, focusing in the end on the utmost significance of finding solidarity and security in relationships with others. In *Watershed,* a 1998 documentary and compilation of interviews and music videos from the Indigo Girls' career, they both remark on the significance of relationships for them, both in their personal lives, and in their songwriting. Emily remarks, "All of 'em are true-story songs." And in further details she describes how her personality emerges in her and Amy's body of work, particularly her priority on relationships. She notes that she can see in her own music, "how important interpersonal relationships are to me. I think about 'em all the time—love relationships, or just how people treat each other—just the whole human intrigue."[14]

One of their most popular songs, "Power of Two," from the 1994 album *Swamp Ophelia*, epitomizes this perspective. The song tells a story of two lovers, and is sung from one to the other, as a song of reassurance. The chorus sings, "we're okay we're fine baby I'm here to stop your crying chase all the ghosts from your head I'm stronger

13. Gen 3:19 NRSV. See also Eccl 3:20, "All go to one place; all are from the dust, and all turn to dust again"; Job 30:19, "He has cast me into the mire, and I have become like dust and ashes" and Job 34:15, "all flesh would perish together and all mortals return to dust" (NRSV).

14. Lambert, *Watershed.*

than the monster beneath your bed smarter than the tricks played on your heart we'll look at them together then we'll take them apart adding up the total of a love that's true multiply life by the power of two." The backdrop of the song is a weekend road-trip, which sets the metaphorical tone of the relationship as a journey. The road is not easy, made obvious by the beginning of the chorus in which the singer promises to stop the other's crying. The third verse continues relating the bittersweet journey: "the closer I'm bound in love to you the close I am to free." The words here relate the difficulty of being in and remaining in relationship, particularly amidst all the other temptations and distractions of the "outside" world. The words allude to marital vows ("for better or worse"). She further plays on the image of a prison, but proclaims that these are not prohibitive bars, but rather, in binding the two of them together, ultimately they set her free. The "power" in the title of the song is not, therefore, a coercive or harmful power, but the power of security, love, and freedom.

The song that is perhaps *the* definitive Indigo Girls' song, if for no other reason than it is their best-known song, is "Closer to Fine." It is the opening track on their 1989 self-titled album. The song is a conversation, and begins with the singer saying to a companion:

> I'm trying to tell you something about my life
> Maybe give me insight between black and white
> The best thing you've ever done for me
> Is to help me take my life less seriously, it's only
> life after all.

The rest of the lyrics follow this sentiment of learning how to best approach life, moving from a dogmatic black-and-white perspective to something more nuanced. The lines that follow speak to taking risk and moving beyond fear, perhaps reminiscent of "The Wood Song" (discussed below). The lyrics communicate a sense of the necessity of risk, and the futility of seeking safety by maintaining a grip on one's fears ("like a blanket"). The revelation comes through the chorus (and perhaps some of the best-known lyrics in the entirety of the Indigo Girls catalog):

> I went to the doctor, I went to the mountains
> I looked to the children, I drank from the fountain
> There's more than one answer to these questions
> pointing me in a crooked line
> The less I seek my source for some definitive
> The closer I am to fine.

Here the song's message is clear, speaking to the fruitless search for ultimate or conclusive truth; instead we ought to be satisfied with the questions, and the variety of answers to questions. Emily remarked on the significance of this song for their catalog:

> ["Closer to Fine"] is about not beating yourself up too hard to get your answer from one place. There's no panacea, that in order to be balanced or feel closer to fine it's okay to draw from this or to draw from that, to draw from a bunch of different sources. So it's about being confused but looking for the answers, and in the end knowing that you're going to be fine. No[t] seeking just one definitive answer.[15]

The song also maintains an implicit critique of ways we attempt to acquire knowledge and answers that may not actually help us arrive at any more secure place: "I spent four years prostrate to the higher mind, got my paper / And I was free," implying that four years of formal, higher education cannot (or did not) teach her everything

15. Wiser, "Emily Saliers."

she hoped to learn, and her self-worth cannot be wrapped up in the grades given to her by someone who perhaps has not actually experienced *living*. This critique is implied in the words: "He never did marry or see a B-grade movie." The third verse offers a comment on the similar futility of "drinking away" one's problems, or otherwise trying to find solidarity or clarity. The chorus repeats three times, the final chorus changing the words:

> We go to the Bible, we go through the workout
> We read up on revival and we stand up for the
>   lookout
> There's more than one answer to these questions
> pointing me in a crooked line . . .

These lines manifest the religious implications most clearly, offering an argument against trying to read any singular, irrefutable interpretation out of any one source. Though those sources can be viewed as authoritative in varying degrees, the song ultimately disputes any notion that a source is authoritative in the *exact same* way for all interpreters and seekers.

The last song on their 2020 release, *Look Long,* acts as a summary statement on their philosophy of life, tipping their hands in the title itself. "Sorrow and Joy" juxtaposes memories both happy and sad. Emily wrote the song for her younger sister, and the song addresses the sister in the past tense—after she has died. The happy memories that blend together with the sorrow of grief propel the song, and the chorus reflects that: "sorrow and joy are not oil and water / They're hater and lover, they inform each other . . . ./in the end we must hold them together." Saliers notes on the writing of the song, "We have to hold these opposites in life. It's the secret, it's the key, it's the way that things are made—by opposing forces that inform each other. I was looking at her [Emily's sister Carrie] photo, thinking how strange it is that when someone dies young, they're forever frozen in your mind as youthful. The contradictory emotion of seeing their vibrancy and knowing that they're gone."[16] The song is a reminder of how life shifts and changes, and though we should not expect time to heal our sorrow, it changes us, it lives inside us and exists alongside our moments of joy—it is both the sorrow and joy *together* that make us human and etch our identities.

Searching for Meaning and Purpose Through Song

One of the most mundane, yet profound ways that all of us engage in theological reflection is in deeper questions of identity, meaning, and purpose. We ask and seek answers to questions such as *What is love? What is a real and honest relationship? Why do we suffer? What is true? What is an authentic life? How do we deal with pain and heartbreak? Why do we deal with pain and heartbreak?* These questions help shape our identities and also help us craft meaning for our lives and our experiences. Questions of meaning and purpose are theological, and it they are the threads of theological reflection woven through so much of the Indigo Girls' catalog.

The final song on *Strange Fire*, "History of Us," continues themes of hope in the midst of despair, light amidst darkness. Emily wrote the lyrics to the song during the summer after she graduated from Emory; she and her family took a trip to Europe. She was inspired, as she "stood in dusty cathedrals and art museums, and at the base of the mighty Alps, filled with awe at the tiny lights of whoever

16. Indigo Girls, "Bio."

dwelled there."[17] The song begins in Paris, the singer addressing some unknown person (though by all indications, a lover or intimate relation of some sort), she says she has gone to "forget your face." There, the structures around her serve as metaphors of the spiritual and relational destruction she feels: "Captured in stained glass / young lives long since passed / . . . / I went all across the continent to relieve this restless love." The rubble around her serves as embodiments of the remains of her love. As she wanders in and out of the gothic cathedrals, she uses the Christian imagery as continued metaphor:

> So we must love while these moments are still
>   called today
> Take part in the pain of this passion play
> Stretching our youth as we must, until we are
>   ashes to dust
> Until time makes history of us.

Here she sees her own life paralleled in the Passion narrative, which could be interpreted as a story of sacrifice, of pain and destruction, but it is called "Passion," because it is also a story of grace, mercy, and love. She continues among the ruins and finds hope: "In the midst of the rubble I felt a sense of rebirth / In a dusty cathedral the living God called / And I prayed for my life here on earth."

At the outset of the song, the landscape serves as a symbol of her own grief and the pieces remaining after her relationship has ended. Here her surroundings continue to mirror her own life, particularly as she transitions from rubble to redemption. She continues to reflect on the setting as it reflects her situation, and has an epiphany: "And it dawns on me the time is upon me / To return to the flock I must keep." The old buildings, faces long-dead and frozen

17. Saliers, *A Year a Month*.

in stained glass, and the decay of the gothic structures initially serve as mere reminders of what the singer has lost. As she looks closer and recognizes the sacred images in the windows and statues, she is reminded of the peace of the "living God," and her prayers change in tone, allowing her to find a sense of resurrection amidst the rubble, which also connects to her language of the "passion play," as the resolution to the biblical passion narrative is also found in resurrection. She concludes her reflections, realizing that her life is not yet over; she has responsibility to others back home, notably using language of sheep—the light is soft and white ("like a lamb") and she must "return to the flock [she] must keep," remembering her own responsibility outside of this temporary brokenness.

A later song, "Free in You," from 2004's *All That We Let In*, sets up the contrast between the singer's perspective on her own and in relationship. She describes, before she "found" this relationship, she felt like a wanderer, without peace of mind. The chorus relates the "after":

> And I'm free in you
> I've got no worries on my mind
> I know what to do
> That's to treat you right
> And love you kind
> Thank you ever on my mind
> Love is just like breathing when it's true
> And I'm free in you.

Again, here in this song, the "after" of finding love, and the security of relationship are framed in terms of safety, security, and freedom.

Another theme that runs through the Indigo Girls' songs is the idea of life itself as a journey. This language is also often used in theological and spiritual conversations about one's "spiritual journey" or "faith journey," the path we take throughout life towards increased understanding of faith, God, and spirituality. For the Indigo Girls this takes on a spiritual connotation, looking at life as a journey and calling into question the idea of fate, and pondering the idea of a specific destination or goal. One such song is from the 1990 album, *Nomads Indians Saints.* "Watershed" begins with these words:

> Thought I knew my mind like the back of my
> hand
> The gold and the rainbow, but nothing panned
> out as I planned.
> They say only milk and honey's gonna make
> your soul satisfied
> Well I better learn how to swim
> 'Cause the crossing is chilly and wide.

She explains that she has been taken by surprise at the course her life has taken. The destination here is not as simple as where she ends up as she has grown older. The language she uses alludes to biblical symbols for the promised land or Heaven. The milk and honey relates to the promise of God to the Hebrew people in Exod 3:8: "and I have come down to deliver them from the Egyptians, and to bring them up out of that land to a good and broad land, a land flowing with milk and honey."[18] God promises that once they reach the promised land (which also symbolizes freedom and power), it will be a land flowing with milk and honey. Further, the "crossing" could allude to the crossing of the Jordan River, which is a significant symbol, first used in Joshua.[19] The image has come to symbolize any major transition, most familiarly in the American slave spiritual,

---

18. NRSV. The phrase is also used in Num 16:13 and Ezek 20:6

19. Cf. Josh 3:1—4:24.

which indicates the final crossing over from this life to eternal life and the ultimate symbol of liberation. The title of the song itself indicates a turning point—a watershed moment—a place in time, a place-marker, after which everything seems (or, in fact, *is*) different. She observes the fragility of life: "Twisted guardrail on the highway, broken glass on the cement / A ghost of someone's tragedy," as she observes signs of other lives cut off too soon, which makes her realize: "How recklessly my time has been spent." All of this has caused her, in a sense, to realize that this moment—or *any* moment—could be a moment that changes everything.

To that point: the lines that include the title of the song spin the "watershed" symbol on its head, claiming that, in reality, any moment could be a watershed moment; any decision we face could be a life-altering decision. What is significant is living our lives honestly, facing our own paths with integrity and intention. The song goes on to address the idea of hindsight and looking back. The singer rejects the notion of regret; obviously, it is easier to see one's own path clearly by looking backwards, but all that is really good for is a "good laugh." The closing line of the song concludes by reiterating the idea that the only fate there is, is the fate we create for ourselves through every decision we make, each one with the potential to create a watershed moment. What becomes most significant is remaining honest to oneself along one's personal path.

Another song from the same album, "World Falls," contains the album's title, *Nomads Indians Saints*. The title connects to their desire to understand life and death—the Ultimates—as explained on *Watershed*. The song is about death, or the fear of the transition from life to death, which is something Amy explains frightens her the most: "I'm not paranoid about natural disasters . . . [but] I can't deal with . . . that split second after you die when your life is leaving your body—I can't deal with that thought. It's not *how* you die; none of that stuff bothers me at all. It's just that split-second thing."[20] In the song she seems paralyzed between the fear of dying and the beauty of living: "This world falls on me with hopes of immortality. / Everywhere I turn all the beauty just keeps shaking me. / I woke up in the middle of the dream, scared the world was too much for me."

She is struck by the beauty of living, and yet finds herself preoccupied with the fear of what happens after death. As Amy explains in the documentary, it is not the *way* she will die that frightens her, but the moment when life leaves her body, what happens then, that paralyzes her. There is a sense in these lyrics that life itself seems so beautiful, so vivid, that it overwhelms her. The song relates Amy's wish to not know so much, so that perhaps she would not be so preoccupied with death. She longs for immortality, so that not only would she not fear death, but that she could also continue to enjoy the beauty of the world.

One of the Indigo Girls' most notable songs, "The Wood Song," comes from *Swamp Ophelia*. Emily describes this "as a kind of Philosophy 101 for myself. Even after all these years, I still think about the words as I sing them and try to live my life by them."[21] "The Wood Song" reflects, much like "Watershed," on life as a journey, with the question of fate, destiny, and conclusive answers at the center. The moment of the song seems to be a frozen moment; life is still, and she is able to look back on her journey. As she

20. Lambert, *Watershed*.

21. From the CD liner notes of *Staring Down the Brilliant Dream*, a live album released in 2010.

reflects, she says, "only the heart that we have for a tool we could use." She realizes that the most important moments and matters of life are those relating to matters of the heart: pain, love, relationship, empathy. The guiding metaphor of the song portrays her and her friends in a boat, which represents their lives together. She describes the boat thusly: "the wood is tired and the wood is old and we'll make it fine if the weather holds." She again echoes the idea discussed above that the most significant and defining parts of life are those lived together and those defined by love, even when it is painful and hard.

As the song continues, we hear a bit more of a spiritual reflection:

> no way construction of this tricky plan was built by other than a greater hand with a love that passes all our understanding watching closely over the journey yeah but what it takes to cross the great divide seems more than all the courage I can muster up inside but we get to have some answers when we reach the other side the prize is always worth the rocky ride.

Here she insists that there is some greater power watching over and guiding her journey. We could interpret this to be God. Although she does not name the "greater hand," she attributes it with a "love that passes all our understanding," thereby alluding to Eph 3:19, " . . . the love of Christ that surpasses all knowledge, so that you may be filled with all the fullness of God," and Phil 4:7, "the peace of God, which surpasses all understanding, will guard your hearts and your minds in Christ Jesus" (NRSV). There is a clear understanding of the divine, informed by Scripture. Emily even notes that she tried—but not all that hard—to speak in veiled terms about her faith: "I can clearly remember wanting to express my belief in God but feeling like maybe I should cloak it a bit . . . Obviously it's not *that* cloaked, as the last part is a direct lift from Philippians 4:7, but I definitely felt trepidation about coming straight out and saying, 'I believe in God and God watches over the journey,'" though that is certainly the belief and message she conveys.[22]

The song also references the "crossing over," as discussed above, the spiritual symbol for a major transition, often the transition from earthly life to eternal life. The song concludes with reflection on the destination:

> sometimes I ask to sneak a closer look skip to
> the final chapter of the book and maybe steer us
> clear from some of the pain that it took to get us
> where we are this far but the question drowns
> in its futility and even I have got to laugh at me
> cause no one gets to miss the storm of what will
> be just holding on for the ride.

The point then of this journey, of the boat ride, is not to know how it will all end, or to even have the ability to know the "right" answers. Rather, the song contradicts that there is any "right" answer or singular destination. "The Wood Song," reflects the philosophy that life is about the journey, the questions, and the fellow companions, not about getting everything right, or being able to know how it will all end up. However, realizing that the journey is guided by incomprehensible love, and the pain that accompanies the love and companionship, make it all worthwhile; they are what define the journey, not the destination. This is certainly not a teleological philosophy. Instead of focusing on the end-goal, the song clearly relates

---

22. Saliers, *A Year a Month*.

a philosophy that places the journey itself, including pain and hardships, as the most significant.

Another song that trades in the life-as-a-journey metaphor comes again from *Swamp Ophelia*. "Least Complicated" echoes the paradoxical sentiment that often the hardest lessons life teaches are, in retrospect, really the easiest to learn—if only we would listen and take heed. The song begins as the singer watches from her window and reflects on life. As she watches children below, she thinks about her former, childlike perspective, when everything seemed quite simple; for every problem, there was a solution. But now she has grown older, and the song also gives us the hint that perhaps she has had her heart broken. Her reflection continues in the chorus: "the hardest to learn was the least complicated." It is a paradoxical realization, akin to the lyrics of "The Wood Song" or "Closer to Fine": that sometimes what we make out to be the most difficult is, in reality, much simpler, and vice versa. Emily notes that the song is certainly autobiographical—she was "two stories above the street" in her house in Atlanta and observed the scene she describes in the song. For her, "the window frames the metaphor-in-motion for the cynicism [she] had mustered up to that time when it came to thinking about love."[23]

Elsewhere Emily has reflected that this song is about her not wanting to be cynical: "I looked down at them, and it looks so easy, and I was just like, you just wait—wait. Because what human beings do is repeat their patterns, oftentimes . . . And the fact that truly, if we could live our lives so much more simply in principle and not repeat the same mistakes, then we'd be happy."[24] Before the final

23. Saliers, *A Year a Month*.
24. Wiser, "Emily Saliers."

chorus, the song ends with a reflection on the necessity of relationship with other people in order to have genuine self-understanding. Though these words also speak to the danger in completely wrapping our self-identity up in other people. All the mirrors leave her confused as to who is the real self. She ends hopeful that she has actually learned from this experience and trusting that she will not have to experience the same pain the next time.

"Deconstruction," from their 2002 album *Become You,* recounts a fight between the singer and a lover, addressing the tricky nature of truth in matters of relationship and love. The fight has had no real closure: "We started a fight that ended in silent confusion." The song goes on to describe what lies at the heart of the anger and hurt; these fights that begin and end in the same place, the all-nighters of arguing and stalemate essentially serve to deconstruct the love that has been built between them. What exactly begins to break down the trust and companionship between them is the individual insistence that truth is non-negotiable, when really, they "get to decide." The song is a bittersweet warning against this destructive situation, setting up the importance of realizing that "truth" is not a bulwark to divide loved ones.

The significance of these types of songs in the Indigo Girls catalog is their witness to the human story. Through these songs, in their narrative, reflection, and assertions, they speak truth to and from human experiences. The Indigo Girls, then, in their music serve as an example of the power of music within the "secular" or "popular" culture to offer a voice out of a particular context. This connects to the essential narrative quality of theology, as addressed particularly by James McClendon and the manifold contextual theologies (e.g., James Cone, Gustavo Gutierrez,

Dorothee Sölle, etc.). Theological reflection, if it is to be genuine and meaningful, tells a story that resonates with lived human experience (the experience of "real people" or "on the ground", as it were), and through the story-telling, resonates with audience members, and in turn communicates something that is *true* in deeply personal and transcendent ways. In the particulars of the stories told in these songs, we find truth spoken to what is common in the universal human experience. They allow for inspirited moments of solidarity and empathy.

In particular, the Indigo Girls' songs of this nature ask questions about things that matter in the day-to-day human life: *What is love? What is a real and honest relationship? Why do we suffer? What is true and honest? How do we deal with pain and heartbreak?* The songs themselves may not *answer* these questions, but they offer a witness to these questions, and it is in offering a sense of solidarity with the human family that the Indigo Girls' music is theological—both in content and in its reflection on human life. Regarding this quality of theological reflection in their music, Emily comments for both her and Amy, "music has compelled both of us to face the truth of how we feel when perhaps we would rather not. Music has exposed our wounds, named our losses, and made us cry. Yet we have also been consoled, comforted, and healed by song."[25] The power of music to serve as an avenue to name truth, wounds, pain, and struggle, and its consonant ability to be a salve for those wounds is deeply theological and spiritual.

Even if (or when) their music does not name "God," or even if in their songs they do not address explicit theological concepts—although much of it does both these

25. Saliers and Saliers, *Song to Sing*, 116.

things—the sum of the emotions, struggles, and reflections expressed through their music remains theological, as Emily concludes: "We want to consider the songlines of human life as pathways along which we human beings find ourselves searching for God."[26] The song that Emily describes as her "most personal song, . . . [because] it talks about my sister's death and the power of a woman's friendship and a loving God," is "She's Saving Me."[27] Her sister, Carrie, died at age 29. The song's chorus alludes to a "hole in my heart," alluding perhaps to a potential cause of her sister's death. The final bridge and chorus of the song blends religious and relational language: "It's not an angry God / It feels like her / It feels like no fear / It feels like no doubt." The song belies the wrestling with grief and the peace of a loving God. As Emily notes, "She's Saving Me," is "a song to my little sister Carrie, and a song to women in my life who held me up; a song to a kind God, not a vengeful God."[28]

A notable song on their holiday album, "There's Still My Joy," illustrates the bittersweet persistence of hope and joy, using the Christmas story as a guiding metaphor. The chorus repeats: "One tiny child can change the world / One shining light can show the way." The moment of the song is after Christmas day, and the singer is seeking "To heal this place inside my heart," and finds hope in the message of the birth of Jesus, the "One tiny child." Resonant with lyrics discussed earlier, "There's Still My Joy," speaks to the reality that joy and pain exist always together, and it is an act of hope to grasp joy in the midst of grieving and sorrow.

26. Saliers and Saliers, *Song to Sing*, 116.
27. Saliers, *A Year a Month*.
28. Saliers, *A Year a Month*.

Two songs from the Girls' 2011 release, *Beauty Queen Sister,* also deal with these themes of meaning and what it means to live authentic human lives. "Birthday Song," is addressed to an old friend (or perhaps a former lover) on their birthday (hence the title). The song reflects on words that the singer can't quite find to say what she wants; she cannot find words to adequately describe her feelings towards the object of the song. Her birthday is a *moment* for her, offering an opportunity to ruminate "Life is short . . . " and acknowledge "the urge is to go / And put something down / That will last." She is mournful as she wrestles with the loss of innocence, permanence, childhood, and spontaneity, yet finds herself resolute to leave her mark, specifically in her relationship with the person turning another year older.

The themes of life being short and time moving ever forward are also reflected in the song "We Get to Feel it All." The song begins with the cliché "My, my—how time flies," and then notes: "I just found my way home." The song is a haunting rumination on the mysteries of life, perhaps even addressed to a larger force: "You set the sun and you hung the moon. / . . . / But if I hold you to my ear, / I can hear the whole world." The title lyric repeats throughout the song, "We get to feel it all," and serves not just as a thread through the song, but has proved to be a guiding philosophy for both Emily and Amy. The beauty, mystery, and even tragedy of life is that we experience the full range of *stuff*—birth, death, sickness, healing, love, pain, heartbreak—the great mystery and gift is that we "get" to live and "feel it all."

A further meditation on youth and aging, "Feel This Way Again," from their 2020 release *Look Long,* is addressed to a younger audience, noting "I know you wanna hurry through your homework / Youth is a hungry beast." Both Amy and Emily have young daughters—Ozilline was born November 2013 to Amy and her partner Carrie Schrader, and Cleo was born November 2012 to Emily and her wife Tristin Chapman—and perhaps this song emerges from observing and parenting girls in the youngest generation. The song instructs, "for today just feel your feelings and hang out with your friends / Because it's never going to feel this way again," providing for the fleetingness of the intensity of youth and, in a way, indulging the drama of young feelings and impulse.

Emily wrote "When We Were Writers," also on their 2020 release, as a tribute to her two years spent at Tulane University, which she refers to as "the two most influential years of my life." The song is a nostalgic ode to the early days of their career: "Amy and I were starting to embark on really what was the beginning of our career . . . Today, we joke about being old, but what is old when it comes to music? We're still a bar band at heart. We are so inspired by younger artists and while our lyrics and writing approach may change, our passion for music feels the same as it did when we were 25-years-old." The song wrestles with their role as "writers," rhyming and saying "when we were fighters . . . igniters." Knowing this is in many ways a retrospective on their decades-long career, one notes the commitment to authenticity in lyrics like "Easy to be cruel better to be kind," and "I've had my day in the sun that's no lie / But I'm still burning inside," noting that with all the ebbs and flows of a successful career in songwriting and performing, the true success is being at this point and recognizing that they still feel the same inspiration and drive as when they begun.

4

What's the Matter Here?

Prophetic Witness and the Indigo Girls

Defining/Describing Prophetic Witness

An examination of the canonized biblical prophets is, it probably goes without saying, a necessary starting point for any project that claims to identify or label something as "prophetic." It would be irresponsible to proceed without due attention to the biblical tradition of the prophets. In general parlance, prophets are often and mistakenly assumed to be something akin to fortune-tellers. But in truth, the biblical prophets were more often engaged in the act of forth-telling, that is, denouncing the way things are, and proclaiming how God intends for the world to be. Their witness also reminds the religious community (most often, of course, in the Bible, Israel), who they are. They do this by re-telling stories of God's faithfulness, like the exodus, and of God's presence, as in the exile.

Abraham Joshua Heschel wrote what remains the seminal work on the biblical prophets. He claims the identity of the prophet is important along with the words proclaimed by him: "The prophet is not only a prophet. He is also a poet, preacher, patriot, statesman, social critic, moralist."[1] Heschel identifies characteristics of prophetic speech throughout the canonized biblical prophets, which can apply to the presence of the prophetic throughout history. The prophet, he reminds us, is situated within a specific point of history, and so his attention is focused on concrete contexts; the prophet denounces specific forms of oppression, and proclaims specific forms of God's redemption.

Using Ezekiel as touchstone, Walter Brueggemann highlights the critical quality of prophetic witness; the prophet is critical of all things fake—including religion and politics: "The key to Ezekiel's proclamation of God is this: *God will not be mocked.* God will not be presumed upon, trivialized, taken for granted, or drawn too close."[2] Therefore prophetic imagination requires prophetic denunciation—speaking out against false gods, false hope, and false schemes of power, dependence, and relationship. Connected to the qualities of denunciation and critique are the ideas of indignation and anger. Heschel aligns these with the divine goals of justice and righteousness. Both justice and righteousness were of utmost concern for the prophets. The kind of justice proffered by the prophets is different than mere legalism, however. According to Heschel, divine "justice dies when dehumanized, no matter how exactly it may be exercised. . . The logic of justice may seem impersonal, yet the concern for justice is an act of love."[3] The prophet proclaims justice with an eye towards

1. Heschel, *Prophets*, xxii.

2. Brueggemann, *Hopeful Imagination*, 53.

3. Heschel, *Prophets*, 257.

divine love. Therefore, what is just is not a blind equality, but rather a sense of *equity* motivated by love for all of creation, and particularly with preference given in support of those without a voice.

Part of the prophetic task is to remind a people of their collective identity; the prophet reminds people of their own story, and reminds them of the God who always stands at the center with the intent to redeem, release from oppression, and empower the powerless. Therefore, Heschel argues, to tell any particular story within history, is to tell One History. Because God is the God of all, what might seem isolated historical moments in actuality connect to the One Story of human history. The unity of the common human narrative according to Heschel must include oppression, pain, and despair, which the prophet includes in her story. The prophet steps in to re-tell the story with a vision towards liberation, healing, and hope. However, Heschel argues, the prophet does not ignore the pain or gloss over the suffering in the service of proclaiming hope.

Brueggemann also addresses the reality of pain and suffering in the work of the prophet. The prophet is creative, and the prophet's work dwells in imagination, but it is always in response to a concrete reality. The hope that emerges out of the prophetic imagination is rendered meaningless if the pain, hurt, and suffering are not taken seriously and accepted as human reality. Brueggeman continues, "Nothing but grief could permit newness. Only a poem could bring the grief to newness."[4] In saying this, not only does Brueggemann highlight the dual significance for the prophetic witness of both a concrete reality and a powerful imagination, but he makes an argument for the necessity of creativity; only through the artistic

4. Brueggemann, *Hopeful Imagination*, 43.

reinterpretation of a distraught and despairing world can hope and newness begin to re-create. A concept that calls to mind the Indigo Girls song "Hand Me Downs," where the "loss of love" is what creates "wholeness."

Brueggemann also identifies the prophetic style with the poetic. Again, calling to mind the imagination of the artist—the poet—and the vision of alternate realities intrinsic to the prophet. In the same way artists reflect the world with a different perspective, or imagine alternative metaphors by which to exist in the world, the prophet reflects a system reconstructed through God's sense of justice, compassion, and power. Brueggemann's poet-prophet invites and "trust[s] other people to continue the image, to finish out of their own experience. But that requires the kind of rich metaphorical language that is open and polyvalent . . . It intends to violate and shatter the categories with which the listener operates,"[5] a shattering echoed in Emily and Don Saliers's insistence on shattering divisions between the sacred and secular. The prophetic imagination is not merely a thing of the ancient past, but rather is the essence of the Holy Spirit that continues to move; it is the ability to remain alive and aware of injustice and unreality, and the imagination to proclaim the hope of a different way to be.

The poet-prophet remains in the ambiguity between exile and homecoming, exile being a "sense of not belonging," and homecoming, "a dramatic decision to break with imperial rationality and to embrace a place called home where covenantal values have currency and credibility."[6] Hence, too, the significance of the prophet as storyteller and the prophet's role in memory is demonstrated; the

5. Brueggemann, *Hopeful Imagination*, 25.
6. Brueggemann, *Hopeful Imagination*, 132.

prophet reminds the community of her identity and cove-
nant with God, and moreover, the prophet, acting through
collective memory, reminds the community "how it was
before . . . this particular set of hopes and fears gained
hegemony."[7] By being part of the community who has been
exiled from their home, from the world as God intended
it, the prophet can also speak for those in the community
who cannot; the prophet speaks honest words about pain
and grief and alienation, yet reminds the community of
the hope and promise of alternative ways of being, through
the divine purpose of love, justice, and grace. Brueggeman
sums it up this way: "*Grief* should permit newness. *Holi-
ness* should give hope. *Memory* should allow possibility . .
. All three affirmations argue that life comes out of death."[8]

Do the prophets need to recognize themselves as prophets to speak prophetically?

In short: no. Brueggemann, further answers this by arguing that there are no limits to expectations as to where
the prophetic spirit of God is proclaimed through "ordinary" persons: "God can 'raise up prophets' and authorize
prophetic voices and deeds in the fullness of God's own
freedom, anywhere, anytime, in any circumstance[;] . . .
prophets are 'naturally' in subcommunities that stand in
tension with the dominant community in any political
economy."[9]

It is helpful to return to Heschel here. He claims that
a prophet "was an individual who said 'No' to his society,
condemning its habits and assumptions, its complacency,

7. Brueggemann, *Hopeful Imagination*, 132.

8. Brueggemann, *Hopeful Imagination*, 132.

9. Brueggemann, *Hopeful Imagination*, xvi.

waywardness, and syncretism. He was often compelled to proclaim the very opposite of what his heart expected. His fundamental objective was to reconcile man [sic] to God."[10] We can take from this that prophets feel compelled to speak, regardless of even being able to accept the message. This addresses the above question in some degree. If prophets do not offer the same interpretation, then we can conclude that the message they proclaim transcends their willingness to embrace their role as such. In other words, they fill the role, and serve as a prophetic witness, even though they likely did not seek the job.

Prophetic Witness as Protest, Dissent, Proclamation

Brueggemann's analysis identifies three primary tasks of prophetic witness. First the prophetic presence offers tools to the community to "confront the horror and massiveness of the experience that evokes numbness and requires denial."[11] Though this rhetoric sounds dramatic, he intends any aspect of life that evokes fear, pain, sorrow, or hopelessness. The prophet then gives us these tools by being a voice for these feelings out of the darkness of human experience. The prophet also speaks using metaphor, thus not only challenging the dominant pattern, even in communication, but provides images, comparisons, and stories to help us find solidarity in our fears and sorrows.

In much the same way that the prophetic task is to be a voice for the pain and suffering and fear of human life, the prophetic imagination is also to bring "public expression [to] those very hopes and yearnings that have

10. Heschel, *Prophets*, xxix.
11. Brueggemann, *Prophetic Imagination*, 45.

been denied too long and suppressed so deeply that we no longer know they are there."[12] Rooted in concrete historical, political, and social context, prophetic witness begins with an honest assessment of the situation, and is able to give voice to the pain, suffering, and fears of the community; from this the prophetic imagination moves to give voice to hope, first remembering the promise of God, and then giving voice and vision to alternatives to the current state of fear, despair, and injustice. It is only through what Brueggemann decisively calls the "action" of the imagination, putting into word, metaphor, poetry, and song, forms of the imagination, that the movement of the prophetic imagination is possible: "The prophet seeks only to spark the imagination of this people, and that in itself turns despair into energy."[13]

Defining the Prophetic Witness

A prophet is someone doing the work of theology, that is, reflecting on the truth of human experience as it relates to the truth of God in hope for renewal and restoration, in the midst of and confronting the world as it is, but does not remain satisfied that the world stay as it is. Hence, prophetic witness is any message—given or received—that speaks honestly out of human experience, relating authentic human struggle, pain, hope, and love, and that denounces injustice and despair. The witness of the prophetic spirit takes on three forms, or characteristics: Protest, Dissent, and Proclamation. These characteristics describe the critical honesty in contexts of fear and despair, and also refer to the proclamation and promise of hope and future

12. Brueggemann, *Prophetic Imagination*, 65.

13. Brueggemann, *Prophetic Imagination*, 77.

contexts of justice, righteousness, and hope given voice through prophetic witness especially via the poetic nature of prophecy.

The political dimension is something that comes in concert with the discography of the Indigo Girls—the element of protest present both in the music itself, but also in the activism of Amy Ray and Emily Saliers. The prophetic witness and imagination manifests itself in the unique ability of musicians to combine deeply personal expression and exploration of themes of humanity, suffering, and redemption, and the impetus toward protest, engaging with the larger community and social systems. Both Amy's and Emily's songwriting offer theological reflection through their storytelling and a sense of solidarity and relationship among fellow human beings. When discussing their work, you cannot ignore the activist projects they have contributed to, started, and advocated for, which they feel are *at least as* important to who they are as their songwriting catalogs. Their activism emerges from a prophetic vision that denounces systems of injustice and proclaims alternative possibilities beyond the status quo. Their work for issues of equality and freedom are important because they emanate from a deeper sense of calling, justice, love, and human solidarity. The question of the artists' biographies is not a trivial one. Without being so bold as to meld the stories of the artists' biographies with the stories they tell through their songwriting, stories remain integral to their work.

Emily and Amy have spoken (in interviews or writings) or sung (in their actual music) of their goal to be honest, to be genuine, and to offer something *real*. This connects to the narrative quality they bring to their music, in that their stories must connect with their audiences as "true" stories; that is, they must connect on a deeper level as authentic retellings of the human experience.

Prophetic Activism: The Indigo Girls

Perhaps the most defining aspect of the Indigo Girls' career (outside of their music, of course) is their activism. Amy Ray and Emily Saliers have taken initiative in working towards various causes defined by their ideals of justice and equality. An overwhelming portion of correspondence to those on their fan email list encourages their audience to join them in these causes. Both are openly queer; though they have had mixed perspectives throughout their career on the importance of their sexuality for their career, gay rights and sexual equality have (not surprisingly) been issues about which they have remained quite vocal. They have not only been involved with issues that affect them personally, however; they have additionally loaned their efforts toward working on issues related to the environment, peace and nonviolence, and indigenous peoples. Particularly during George W. Bush's two terms as president, they expressed concern regarding the war in Iraq, and worked towards peace. All of their activism ultimately relates to their understanding of justice and equality, rooted in both their clear views on social justice, mercy, and peacekeeping and peacemaking. This activism manifests in their music, their own personal endeavors to get fans involved, as well as their personal activity while "off duty," so to speak.

For both Ray and Saliers their activist work is *at least as* important to them and defining as their identity as folk-rock songwriters. While they have certainly gained a larger audience and platform from which to speak on behalf of their causes *because* they are musicians, they have a difficult time compartmentalizing the two in terms of their calling—their most important work or most significant contribution. In one interview, Emily said, "Our music and activist work are married. We've used our music and shows to provide education and information and if people are interested in it and want to take part, that's great."[14] Amy also has remarked: "I'm torn between being most proud of our social justice work or most proud of our music."[15] Their intertwined lives as musicians and activists also share an equally long history; Amy recalls, "one of the first ways we got involved in activism was to do a benefit for the Open Door Community, a group who is still serving the homeless and folks in prison for over 30 years."[16]

Although not every issue on behalf of which they work may personally affect them (at least not obviously), they feel intimately involved and invested in all parts of it. This personal investment derives from a deeply-ingrained sense of solidarity and community across cultures, ages, and demographics. As Emily remarks, "Just because you're not from someone's neighborhood doesn't mean that you can't empathize and relate to their issues, make the connections to your own issues, and to national and international issues, and try to be part of the change." This sense of empathy and solidarity is something they hope to pass along to their fans, or beyond that, Emily continues, they believe their fans expect from them: "[O]ur fans obviously know that we're activists, they know we have this long history of marrying our music with our activism, so they expect it from us."[17]

14. Hubbard, "Interview: Indigo Girls."
15. Hubbard, "Interview: Indigo Girls."
16. Ray, *A Year a Month.*
17. Schulz, "Let It Be Me."

Their audience certainly has grown to expect and appreciate activism and advocacy as part of the Indigo Girls "experience"—their website has a dedicated page for "Activism,"[18] which is organized categorically: Peace, Justice, & Human Rights; Women's Health/HIV/AIDS; Native & Environmental; Queer; Independent Media; Music Community; and Voter Education. The Activism page also includes sections on Honor the Earth (an organization they co-founded in 1993), Georgia & the South, and links to previous writings and accounts of their "Activist Journeys" to Cuba, Chiapas, and "Summer of '05 Political Wrap Up."

The Indigo Girls have grown to expect something in return from their audience and fan-base. They release frequent appeals to join them in their causes, sometimes through basic education about different issues, sometimes implorations to contact senators and representatives regarding other political issues. During campaign years they encourage fans to register and make a plan to vote: "We hope you will get involved in your communities—educating yourself, getting out the vote, and heading to the polls on November 4 [2008]."[19] Additionally, they will work with organizations to have booths at their concerts to assist audience members who might not be registered to vote. They have also brought their activism on tour with them, asking their ticket-holders to contribute in addition to enjoying their live shows. On one recent tour, they sponsored a food drive at each concert, partnering with Rock for a Remedy and local food banks to provide food in the communities. Animal rights and wellbeing are also important to both Saliers and Ray, so in addition to the food drive, they worked

18. Indigo Girls, "Activism."

19. Indigo Girls, " 2008–05–20: Election 2008."

"with animal rescue groups and pet food banks to organize a collection of pet food at concerts . . . We believe everyone's bowl should be full!"[20] More recently, when the CO-VID-19 pandemic forced them to cancel tour dates, they pivoted to online streaming concerts, and raised money for Honor the Earth and Feeding the Valley (food banks and food insecurity outreach in rural areas of Georgia and Alabama), as well as using their platforms to encourage people to follow science, stay home, wear masks, and generally help take care of themselves and each other during the pandemic.[21]

By most accounts, this piece of their activism—involving fans and concert attendees—is quite successful. Amy wrote amidst the 2009 tour, "The food drive is gaining momentum and at this point we have collected nearly two tons of food plus financial donations to distribute an additional 28 tons more. You are really all doing your part."[22] In almost every piece of correspondence emailed from either Emily or Amy (or both), they include a line of conviction and encouragement, entreating listeners to also work towards common goals of peace, justice, and equality. For example, a line from a letter from Amy Ray: "I am wishing you luck out there and hoping you feel up to an engagement with the world. We need you right now."[23] While they are aware of the greater presence their higher-profile affords them, they believe that everyone has something to contribute and everyone ought to contribute in order to change the world. The activism they engage in, promote, and lend their voices to is as much a part of who they are

20. Ray and Saliers, "Note . . . March 24, 2009."
21. Paste Magazine, "Happiest Hour."
22. Ray, "May 29, 2009."
23. Ray, "April 8, 2003."

as Amy Ray and Emily Saliers—and together as the Indigo Girls—as their music and lyrics. According to Amy their activism is "part of the tapestry of our year and our music, giving us even more energy to travel, play songs, promote the records, and gather more resources for our goals."[24] As this section moves forward to more specific issues, we will look first to interviews and writings; examples from the Indigo Girls' musical catalog will buttress the discussion of the particular areas of activism. The following sections are organized in the same order as the activism section of their website.

Peace, Justice, Human Rights

Peace

Though it is often an implicit concern in their writings, both Emily and Amy are fiercely anti-war and anti-violence, advocating for peace and political policies that focus on peace-making and community building. They adamantly criticize any domestic or international policy that they feel breeds and feeds an imperialistic and/or militaristic mindset. Though most often expressed through their music, building peace and resisting violence remains central to their understanding of justice. Both have visited Fort Benning, Georgia, to join the protests against the School of the Americas. In 2006, following just such a trip, Emily reflected on that experience, offering a poignant insight into her understanding of peace and justice:

> I attended the School of Americas' protest on November 19th . . . The weather was cold and crisp and, once again the gathering was an inspiring

24. Ray, *A Year a Month.*

63

group of thousands and thousands from all over who came to sing, to pray, to remember, and to shut down this school at Ft. Benning that teaches torture, death, and destruction. One of the most powerful things about this protest gathering is the wide variety of groups and people who attend, not only to protest, but to actually sing the names of those who have been tortured, murdered, or disappeared in Latin America. There are atheists and anarchists and agnostics and socialists, communists, capitalists, and Christians and Jews from different congregations and synagogues. There are people from all walks of faith. There are community groups, grandmothers, and individuals that claim no affiliation but that a member of the human family, concerned about all of our brothers and sisters. When such diverse groups of people and individuals come together—groups that might, for lack of understanding be at odds with each other—to unite in a common cause, I truly feel in my bones that the world can change for the better. That we can lay down our weapons and engage in dialogue and promote peace through a desire to see human dignity full recognized. Through our activism we embrace the sacredness of life.[25]

Like most Americans, September 11, 2001, served as a watershed moment for Ray and Saliers. Instead of responding with fear or seeking vengeance, they responded with an even deeper desire for peace: "9/11 brought issues closer to home. For me emotionally it was a stronger response to violence and a more impassioned prayer for peace and just a stronger belief that we all take part in what we all do in the world. Like the large dysfunctional

25. Saliers, "12.05.06."

communities and nations. So I feel stronger about working for peace."[26]

One of the most poignant songs related to issues of warfare is "Our Deliverance," from the 2002 album, *Become You*. The song remains important to the Indigo Girls, as Emily reflected a few months after 9/11 (2001): "We've been playing 'Our Deliverance' live a lot and wanting peace and bringing everyone closer together . . . that song is very poignant to me."[27] The song begins by describing a sense of loss and confusion, and offers a glimmer of hope for "deliverance." Emily notes the song "started as a love song and ended up being an anti-war song."[28] The opening lines utilize landscape as a founding image for the coming critique: "Now we can say that nothing's lost and only change brings round the prophecy / Where now it's melting, the solid frost was once a veil on greener landscapes we would see." The song begins on a personal note before it broadens the scope to a cultural and political level; the initial perspective of loss and introspection seems focused on a lost relationship. With the first chorus, the scope moves outward, the "deliverance" is universal, and it centers, as we have seen before in Indigo Girls' songs, on love. The song continues toward a political and military focus, as the perspective shifts ever broader:

> They're sending soldiers to distant places
> X's and O's on someone's drawing board
> Like green and plastic but with human faces
> And they want to tell you it's a merciful sword.

Though this song was written and the album released prior to the start of the Iraq war in March 2003, the United

26. Ray and Saliers, "Web Chat."

27. Ray and Saliers, "Web Chat."

28. Saliers, *A Year a Month*.

States' troops were already waging war in Afghanistan, the rhetoric of "war on terror" was rife during Bush's years in office, and the US already had a history, prior to George W. Bush's foreign policy, of invading other countries under the "merciful" guise of liberty, democracy, and stability. Amy criticizes these motivations: "Just as we promised a new life of democracy and Christianity to the Native Americans, we are promising a new democracy to the Middle East. I am not the first one to say that this analogy can only go so far. After all Saddam Hussein is no upstanding Native American leader . . . But our good intentions certainly do have an agenda and that agenda is oil."[29] Though these reflections are offered in the context of environmental policy, it's all a common refrain that whatever the "cause," violence and war remain unacceptable means to a desired end. The song furthers this sentiment:

> But with all the blood newly dried in the desert
> Can we not fertilize the land with something else
> There is no nation by God exempted
> Lay down your weapons and love your neighbor
>   as yourself.

The assessment is not based on policy or politics, but rather it is couched in terms of religion, hinting at the words of scripture to "Love your neighbor as yourself,"[30] and Jesus' admonition to Peter to "put your sword back."[31] The song ends with words of cautious hope, resting on faith and love.

Two other songs that address issues of political war and violence include "Everything in Its Own Time," from *Shaming of the Sun,* and "Tether," from *All that We Let In.* The latter is an anthemic plea to "true believers" for unity

29. Ray, "Letter," April 2003.
30. Lev 19:18; Mark 12:31.
31. John 18:11.

and understanding. Comparable to "Become You," (discussed below), the song relates a struggle with a tattered (to say the least) past. It opens with a clear reference to abolition of slavery, indicating a further struggle with a Southern history:

> Whatever it was, it wasn't manumission[32]
> To spill the blood, to pull the weed
> You can bury the past, but it's a mausoleum
> With the ghost of a fist that won't let us be.

The persistent question, hoping for unity or reconciliation of some sort, is then voiced: "Can we bring it together, / Can we call from the mountain to the valley below? / Can we make it better,/ Do we tether the hawk, do we tether the dove?" The song hopes for a better future, yet sees clearly a past that has been shoved down or brushed aside. Observing that history here has been swept under the proverbial rug, the singer does not rest optimistically. The song title emerges as it references "hawks" and "doves," the classic contrast between those who would wage war and those who seek peace.

The singer retells a conversation with a neighbor: "He said, 'We need a few less words dear, we need a few more guns.'" The struggle at the heart of the song is revealed in this conversation; the singer expresses concern for the society around her, and her neighbor answers by suggesting further violence.[33] In response, she expresses doubt: "But will it bring us together?" The rhythm and key of the

32. Manumission is the freedom or enfranchisement of slaves *by their owners,* as opposed to emancipation, which involves government action.

33. In some ways this echoes the rationale for owning handheld weapons: "the best way to stop a bad guy with a gun is a good guy with a gun."

song shift, as the vocals belt out: "Enduring love / Why so much and so strong, beyond this short existence? / So don't be still," here shifting to the plea for others to join in. The shift here calls on a higher ideal, "enduring love," which is something the Indigo Girls (particularly Emily) have emphasized in their words. Both in music and otherwise, they highlightthe centrality of love to lead to genuine transformation, whether it be personal, political, or social (a distinction that, they would say, is nearly impossible to make). There is, in these lines, an eternal significance, an insistance that hope, peace, and love endure long past our "short existence." The singer continues to argue that the fight is not futile or lost and it is not only an individual struggle to make the world better (not over!); it requires other people. The song concludes with a call to "true believers," the most significant piece to the song's plea, because the call portrays trust and reliance on a critical mass of others who believe in the power of love and the potential for all those of like mind to join in tethering the hawks of war, to be fed by hope, and to let "enduring love" change the course of things.

The more abstract tone of "Everything in Its Own Time" is accompanied by lyrics that assume the voice of a parent, teacher, or some other authority figure: "Remember everything I told you . . . " Though the song opens with the instruction to "remember" and repeats this a few times, we are not yet clued in to what has been told or taught. The singer says, "Remember everything I told you, . . . what was once your pain will be your home," indicating that something is not right and there is a need to remember words of instruction or wisdom. We are given some insight as to what this might be: "All around the table the white-haired men have gathered Spilling their sons' blood like table wine Remember everything in its own time . . . Boys around the table mapping out their strategies Kings all of mountains one day dust." The central criticism is directed at those plotting and planning war, particularly those sending others to fight the wars they strategize, far removed from the trauma and violence they plot.

The song plays with titles, saying that the men are planning the wars in which their own sons will die, perhaps not necessarily their literal sons, but using the relational terms to illustrate the intrinsic kinship of all human beings, an idea that remains central to the Indigo Girls' theology and philosophy. Their use of "Boys" and "Kings" reveals a deeper critique about the transiency of the people and their plans. By first using "men", and then juxtaposing that with "boys around the table," the song demonstrates the parallel between boys playing war games, and men plotting real war. It should be observed, too, the hint towards eucharistic imagery of the sons' blood spilling, "like table wine," an illustration of the sacrifice and, perhaps, atonement in and through their deaths.

Following this observation, we hear what it is that the singer has been told: "A lesson learned a loving God and things in their own time . . . But this poverty is our greatest gift The weightlessness of us as things around begin to shift." The lesson here echoes the wisdom-teacher's instructions from Ecclesiastes on the fleetingness of time and relationship, particularly within the realm of our own temporal lives and the eternal God. The title of the song itself connects to the best-known passage from Ecclesiastes, which insists, "For everything there is a season, and a time for every matter under heaven."[34] The words in the song point to the passing quality of even war and violence, and

34. Eccl 3:1.

yet the eternality of a "loving God," which echoes further the words from Ecclesiastes: "Moreover I saw under the sun that in the place of justice, wickedness was there, and in the place of righteousness, wickedness was there as well. I said in my heart, God will judge the righteous and the wicked, for he has appointed a time for every matter, and for every work."[35] The lyrics, in critiquing a culture of violence where those who sit around tables plan war, like boys playing games, in essence serve as a reminder of the temporality of all the power we seek ("Kings of all mountains one day dust"), the possessions we seek to collect ("We own nothing, nothing is ours"), even our pain ("What was once your pain will be your home"); what the singer does know is the truth of "a loving God," and that is antidote enough to the brokenness elsewhere observed.

"Leeds" from *Shaming of the Sun,* confronts political ignorance and blindness to social and cultural violence and injustice. The song sets up an image of churches along the skyline, though the religious icon serves as a symbol of silence and impotence. The sun is setting, and the sky is allowing the darkness to set in, and as that happens, "the steeples pierce the skylight till the last of it bleeds." The description is significant in the parallel it sets up: violence juxtaposed with religious imagery, made even more poignant by the steeple that is a cross, the instrument upon which Jesus himself bled and died. The perspective of this song is the singer in a hotel room looking out her window. She describes herself as "Well-fed and halfway drunk," and then seems fixated and anxiety-ridden, the nightly news epitomizing the sources of her anxiety and stress: "Sixteen black churches burning on the TV all the way from Texas to Tennessee a politician locks my eye and says to me

35. Eccl 3:16–17.

there is no crisis here there's no conspiracy." Here leveling a critique against meaningless violence and the political impotency or even conspiratorial cover-up of the reality and extent of that violence. She takes all of this personally, allowing it to affect her emotional state: "anxiety over a deep dark drop down into nothingness." Though from 1997, this willful misrepresentation and distortion of the truth seems even more poignant now some twenty-five years later..

Two songs from *Beauty Queen Sister* further develop the Indigo Girls' commitment to peace in the face of violence and warfare. "Feed and Water the Horses," uses the singer's dreams as a framework to reflect on larger themes. The reality is she feels as though there is so much that is left unresolved in her life, and those things are haunting her "dark heart of [her] dark sleep." The second verse considers broad sweeps of history, "Once there were wars fought over spice and salt . . . ," reflecting, with hindsight, we can see how trivial it is to kill over such things. The verse continues, "Nothing much has changed in this modern age," mourning the reality that the reasons we go to war now will seem equally trivial in the future (if they do not already seem so).

Amy wrote "War Rugs" following the Arab Spring protests and uprisings, with Egypt specifically named: "Young Egypt seized the moment / And brought that bastard down." On their album *Live with the University of Colorado Symphony Orchestra,* the "War Rugs" performance is dedicated to the people in the Middle East, as noted in the album's liner notes. The song's title parallels traditional Muslim prayer rugs. The rest of the lyrics demonstrate a wrestling with the fraught relationship we in the West have with Arabic nations and governments: "We treated you like hunters / Until you kicked the goal / Now we're claimin' you for our team." Further, the song reflects a wrestling with the question of when violence and warfare might be a necessary means to an end; the Arab Spring rebellions were the culmination of decades upon decades of fascist and oppressive governments coming to a head in a zeitgeist of social unrest and protest, yet were also incredibly violent. "War Rugs," ends with the reflection turning inward, the singer perhaps wanting to identify with the people in the Middle East: "I want to understand / The soul it takes to stand / For something bigger than / Myself."

Following the shooting at Marjorie Stoneman Douglas High School in Parkland, Florida, CNN aired a Town Hall meeting that included student-survivors, parents, and Florida Senator Marco Rubio and NRA spokesperson Dana Loesch. Amy Ray recalls, "I was struck by these citizens' willingness to meet and try in earnest to have a dialogue between the two sides."[36] She wrote "Muster," from their 2020 release, as "a frank accounting of the American gun-violence epidemic."[37] The song seems to be addressed to young people: "then we saw the kids and found ourselves saying / We're gonna make it up to you / . . . / We're gonna get this right." In a country that too quickly offers its "thoughts and prayers," Ray asks, "Is this the best we could muster? / Custer or just prayers for the slain / I wanna get this right and not the same ole thing." As the song develops, the concern widens to realities of violence for children all over the world, referring to poverty, hunger, and specifically naming Yemen. Speaking to a young student (perhaps her daughter): "It's your first lock down, you're so young / But so are the kids under the barrel bombs / It's the

36. Indigo Girls, "On Their 16th Studio Album."
37. Indigo Girls, "Biography—Despite Our Differences."

evil we helped let loose, it's what we've become / It's all a gun." The song embraces the ubiquity of violence, and globalizes it, arguing that we cannot separate violence in our schools from bombs in the street in countries across the world—it's a universal, global problem. The song stands as a lament against the pervasive human fetishizing of guns and violent impulses to solve problems, noting that it is not a solution at all.

Justice and Human Rights

Through their music the Indigo Girls build upon the theological idea of community-building and solidarity-forming in order to tell stories, to relate the authentic experience of human struggle and reconciliation, of human love and pain. Further, they work outward, convicted that their music and songwriting is an avenue to speak truth to power. All of this serves as theological reflection worked out in public and vocal forms of prophetic denunciation and proclamation. In ways beyond what has already been discussed, their songs take on this prophetic tone of denunciation—speaking against oppression, inequality, and injustice.

The song "Money Made You Mean," from *Despite Our Differences,* takes on economic injustice in its biting criticism of how money changes people and priorities. The song takes on the culture of cultivated need and greed that takes hold in our acquisition-driven economy. The title comes from the assessment that money and the insatiable drive for more turns people mean. The first two verses accuse and then ask: "How much do we really need?" The "meanness" caused by money here is related to selfishness; the singer claims the person being addressed will "challenge and defend" not noble causes, but rather likely the right and ability to preserve what (s)he has. The question at the heart is a matter of need, but the singer is clearly not impressed with the question: "But where did it come form in the first place?" This goes much deeper than the possession of money, and includes the system perpetuated by money changing hands without actually fixing a broken system. In turn this system creates greedy, mean purveyors of wealth. What is the answer, then? Amy suggests that, although money often does create perceived needs and spreads greed, she does not feel that money itself is the problem: "money is a tool that can also do good. In the song, I'm asking that questions about myself in a cynical sort of way. As an activist, you can do good with it, but that still drives you to want more money and that drive can take over the good."[38] The song, then, is as much a self-critique as an external one, serving as a reminder of the danger of accruing wealth and getting caught up in a system that encourages consumption and individual gain. Instead, Amy and Emily focus on their message of relationship, solidarity, and sharing.

There are plenty of songs that have been written not just to critique, but to inspire, to motivate, to urge listeners to act, to work for change, equality, and justice. From *Come on Now Social*, "Go" is a song true to their rock-and-roll roots, acoustically speaking. The song opens the album and wastes no time getting to the point, describing her own genealogy of protest and oppression: "Grandma was a suffragette / Blacklisted for her publication / Blacklisted for my generation." The song describes a history of inequality and discrimination, referring to suffragettes within her own lineage, those who fought, argued, and worked

38. Kinkaid, "Amy Ray and Emily Saliers."

for the enfranchisement of women. It links this history to her own situation, implying that current generations are not divorced from history; in fact, by saying that her grandmother was blacklisted for "[her] generation," she recognizes the persecution her grandmother's generation faced was for the sake of not only contemporary peers but also for all future generations. The song then shifts focus, provoking others to "Go Go Go," working for similarly-minded goals:

> Raise your hands
> Raise your hands high
> Don't take a seat
> Don't stand aside
> . . . I know you kids can stand the rain
> I know the kids are still upsetters
> Cause rock is cool but the struggle is better

The remaining verses are a struggle and invective against apathy. The song encourages listeners to act similarly to previous generations when confronted with messages and systems of inequality and injustice. The lyrics here speak out against the information often communicated by those comfortably in power, or those who might stand to lose if significant populations "Don't take a seat" or "stand aside." The song unswervingly denounces implications that one is "too old" or "too young" to matter or to effect change. It also grapples with arguments against change. To the stance that "it's always been done that way," it asks "Did they tell you it was set in stone[?]" And in questioning the idea "That you'd end up alone," they rattle the notion that in speaking out against injustice or oppression one might be left to speak alone, which fosters fear by keeping people silent. The song itself serves a dual purpose: to remind listeners of a history of social change that is, in fact personal (made clear by connecting it to the singer's family), and to motivate listeners towards similar action, boldly unafraid of consequences.

Amy Ray has also enjoyed a successful solo career, and while I dare not try to incorporate all songs from her three albums into this conversation, one song seems too poignant to ignore. From her solo album, *Prom*, released in 2005, "Let It Ring" is a fast-driving song cheering on those who speak up for causes of justice and equality, while also indicting those who perpetuate hate. Amy wrote the song following the 2004 March for Women's Lives, for which the Indigo Girls performed. Discouraged—angered, even—by the people who protested against the march, "especially the young kids holding a mixture of hateful pro-life and anti-gay signs," Amy wrote the song as an answer to "their fear-mongering message of intolerance and bigotry, which was being sold as Christianity,"[39] a message clear in the opening lines:

> When you march stand up straight.
> When you fill the world with hate
> Step in time with your kind and
> Let it ring
> When you speak against me
> Would you bring your family
> Say it loud pass it down

The lyrics clearly parallel the prophetic speech of Martin Luther King Jr., particularly in his "I Have a Dream Speech," wherein he repeats "Let freedom ring," several times.[40] In the language, Ray sets up a denunciation of those who speak against her, and those who enable hate–fueled contexts. She confronts the "other," asking that they

39. Ray, *A Year a Month.*
40. King, "I Have a Dream."

be open about their hate and condemnation, including even their families; the indictment takes on a religious tone, proposing to speak from their perspective: "Let it ring to Jesus 'cause he sure'd be proud of you / You made fear an institution and it got the best of you / Let it ring in the name of the one that set you free." The chorus picks up on the religious overlap in hate speech, particularly against homosexuality in America.[41] She then uses the pattern from the first verses and chorus to explain herself:

> As I wander through this valley
> In the shadow of my doubting
> I will not be discounted
> So let it ring
> You can cite the need for wars
> Call us infidels or whores
> Either way we'll be your neighbor
> So let it ring

Religious motivation and justification are on her side. She alludes to the twenty-third psalm, which is often used to remind people of God's presence, particularly in times of loss and fear. She responds to the "haters" by claiming that she and others like her remain their "neighbor," regardless of their continued efforts to squash them.[42] The use of the word neighbor here is significant, as it continues the

---

41. Following the defeat of Proposition 8 in California, many accused the Church of Latter-Day Saints (whose population is largely concentrated in Utah) of conspiring and channeling money toward the campaign against the legislation. Likewise, Westboro Baptist Church in Kansas is notorious for their outspoken anti-gay stance, which is manifest in protesting in various situations with signs that read "God Hates Fags." It is well-documented that a significant bloc against homosexuality (including gay marriage; repealing Don't Ask, Don't Tell; and embracing homosexuality as an acceptable "lifestyle"), are religious, particularly Evangelical Christian.

42. See also, Rom 12:20–21.

religious themes in the song. After all, Jesus declared that the second greatest commandment is to "love your neighbor as yourself," repeating the words from Leviticus that commanded the same thing.[43] The song, therefore, turns the religion of those who perpetuate hate and war back on them, illustrating their hypocrisy and failure to follow the commands of Jesus, whom they claim is on their side. The song concludes by bolstering up those who work for freedom, justice, and equality: "And the strife will make me stronger / As my maker leads me onward," claiming righteousness for their side too: "I'm gonna let it ring to Jesus / Cause I know he loves me too / And I get down on my knees and I pray the same as you." She claims the same justification, and we get the sense that she believes her cause is the true cause of righteousness, in its understanding of "neighbor" and proclaiming equality—both on earth and before God—and claiming an eschatological freedom for all.

Implicit in many of their lyrics, the song "Rise of the Black Messiah," on *Beauty Queen Sister,* takes on racial injustice, particularly the significant disparities of incarceration rates between black men and any other demographic in the United States. The song was written by Amy and was inspired by a letter she received from Herman Wallace, one of the "Angola Three." Wallace, along with two other men, was convicted of killing a prison guard and spent 41 years in solitary confinement. He maintained his innocence and was freed in 2013, after a judge ruled he had not received a fair trial back in 1974. He died two days after his release. Wallace had written Amy a letter asking her to tell his story, and this song is the result. She says that she wanted to honor him "and every other soul that's

43. Matt 19:19, cf. Lev 19:18.

been crucified by the system of mass incarceration and the racism of our broken criminal justice system."[44] The song draws connections between slavery, Jim Crow, and mass incarceration, an even clearer thread given that Wallace and the rest of the Angola Three were confined in a prison complex whose grounds used to be a Southern, slave-labor dependent plantation. The song title comes from the CIA and FBI's efforts to squelch Wallace and the other men's organizing (they had joined the Black Panthers while in prison), noting: "They called you the rise of the black messiah and said they'd do any damn thing they could to keep ya—." The song levels the critique against federal authorities who wanted to prevent the Angola Three and other black men "from spreading the word, the gospel of freedom and the black man's worth." Amy notes Wallace's story and his letter to her were so hopeful and inspiring that she wanted to sing for him because of "in the face of that [solitary confinement] to still have faith in humanity" spoke to a depth of hope she could hardly fathom.

Women's Heath/HIV/AIDS

In keeping with the categories on the Indigo Girls *Activism* section, this section of our discussion considers songs that address gender inequality. This piece of their activism is certainly wrapped up with their queer activism, which will be discussed at length below, but there are a few songs worth discussing separately here. Several of their songs take on women's issues directly, others include passing references to sexuality and gender as the hot-button political and social issue that it is. Two examples of songs that address issues of gender and sexism include "Pendulum

44. Indigo Girls, "Black Messiah—Behind the Scenes."

Swinger" (from 2006's *Despite Our Differences*) and "Virginia Woolf" (from 1992's *Rites of Passage*). "Virginia Woolf" subtly takes on the idea of gender, primarily in terms of the struggle of a female artist. The song tells the story of the singer reading the writings of Virginia Woolf more than a century later and feeling an intimate connection to the author. Woolf is perhaps best known for her work *A Room of One's Own* (to which the song refers in the lines: "they published your diary and that's how I got to know you a key to the room of your own and a mind without end"), which contains the assertion, "a woman must have money and a room of her own if she is to write fiction."[45] By reading Woolf's words, the singer feels she has, in some sense, gained her own salvation: "here's a young girl on a kind of telephone line through time the voice at the other end comes like a long-lost friend so I know I'm alright . . . I just got a letter to my soul . . . you say each life has its place." Woolf, a prolific author, struggled with her own identity as a female writer and with mental illness, until she ended her own life at the age of 59. The singer finds through Woolf's writing a sense of solidarity and companionship. She sings to Woolf: "but if you need to know that you weathered the storm of cruel mortality a hundred years later I'm sitting here living proof," assuring the dead writer that her life, though clearly tormented and without peace, served a greater good, even if through the life of this one reader.

As the song continues, she reflects on this author–reader relationship: "[you] sent your soul like a message in a bottle to me and it was my rebirth so we know it's alright life will come and life will . . . " Though the song does not address gender inequality or sexism specifically,

45. Woolf, *Room of One's Own*, 2.

80

by relating to the life and work of a female author who struggled with similar issues of gender identity as an artist, the song speaks to the need for community, for shared understanding, and for the possibility of transformation. The singer realizes a truth about human, and more specifically women's experience that stretches across centuries and rejects the despair.

The song alludes also to the importance of female friendship and mentorship. Throughout their career, Emily and Amy have sought out, developed, and cultivated community–especially with artists and other music professionals. When describing the creation of their albums on their Tumblr blog, they both put a great deal of emphasis on all the people who contributed and helped birth each project into its final form. Never is the process described with the cold precision of business, but with warmth, excitement, and a genuine sense of a village that is required to get from songs to produced album. Beyond that, they tell the stories of their careers through the lens of collaboration. Collaboration and sharing has been part and parcel of who they are. As Amy tells it, "We grew up in community and believe that everything should be done that way: activism, playing, etc."[46] In fact, Amy's own record label emerged from just such an impetus. She founded Daemon Records in 1990, just after the Indigo Girls got their first major record deal, out of her own sense of fandom: "I'm a fan, I have this money, I've got all these friends that can't afford to make records, so I'm going to funnel my money into that."[47] She was not motivated by capitalistic intentions of profiting off her own corner of the music business, rather

---

46. Tongson, "Amy Ray."
47. Tongson, "Amy Ray."

she wanted to provide space and opportunity for those in her community to make music.

The song "Pendulum Swinger," different from "Virginia Wolff," takes on sexism directly, as an institutional manifestation of inequality. While the song is primarily about sexism, it also addresses "what the Girls view as President Bush's wrongheaded approach to the war on terrorism."[48] The song is a conversation between two friends. The singer has met a friend for coffee, and she is frustrated: "I got a bad case I can't shake off of me." She has sought out her friend for some counsel, or perhaps hope: "You work in the system / You see possibilities and your glistening / Eyes show the hell you're gonna give 'em / When they back off the mic for once and give it to a woman." The singer perhaps seems confounded because she observes the world and is left with "the fevered walking round wondering how it ought to be," and yet her friend who is part of the "system" (Emily relates later that this is a true story and the friend is a clergy member[49]), seems to remain hopeful and full of possibilities. This friend believes in a future when women will have the opportunity to speak from a position of power as part of the "system." The song levels a direct critique of religion as it relates to women (or has neglected to do so, as it were): "But they left out the sisters / Praying to a father god so long I really missed her / . . . / But you can't keep a spirit down that wants to get up again." There is criticism of institutional religions (in an initial reference to Sanskrit) throughout the song, but most specifically Christianity, naming especially Roman Catholicism, for leaving out women's voices and glossing over women's experiences. Emily explains the feeling behind the lyrics:

48. Indigo Girls, "Biography—Despite Our Differences."
49. Wiser, "Emily Saliers."

"[The song] takes on the patriarchy in the church, and the squelching of women's voices in power within organized religion . . . The language of organized religion so often is so male–oriented, the male pronouns, . . . and it's all male, male, male. So part of that song is about I miss the goddess. I miss the balance of female/male spirits both together."[50] The symbol of the pendulum swinger functions as an emblem of hope that the patterns, systems, and powerful will shift and swing back in another direction; for the purposes of the imagination at play in this song, women are the ones who will swing the pendulum back, undoing and redeeming injustices and inequalities: "The epicenter of love is the pendulum swinger / She is, she is, she is."

Because the song addresses inequalities, particularly at the hands of institutions and systems, it almost necessarily broaches political power and control. The album was released in 2006; the song was likely penned during or shortly after George W. Bush's re-election, and several years into both the wars in Iraq and Afghanistan. The song, then, as Saliers explains, is also "about the Bush Administration and his macho posturing and the bull-whip and the gunslingers and all that, like hawks, war hawks."[51] The song, as much as it is about women and religion, opens up much more than that, becoming a song about institutionalized violence, control, and the improper uses of such power. This is illustrated by the following verse: "What we get from your war walk / Ticker of the nation breaking down like a bad clock / I want the pendulum to swing again / So that all your mighty mandate was just spitting in the wind." "Pendulum Swinger" links institutionalized violence and systems of sexism as parts of an unjust whole

50. Wiser, "Emily Saliers."
51. Wiser, "Emily Saliers."

83

that requires the metaphorical pendulum to swing away from patriarchy, heteronormative violence, and problem-solving using armed conflict. This swing depends on what, for Saliers, is summed up simply as love: "And my belief is that we have to come from a place of love in order to heal the world. So in order for the pendulum to swing back the other way, away from war and violence and death and desecration, is to come from a place of love."[52] Hence, the crux of the song, which proclaims, "the epicenter of love is the pendulum swinger." She emphasizes this idea in reflecting on the political overtones of the song: "you're not gonna win this with a bullwhip or posing with your hands on your hips like Mr. Tough-Guy President. The only way to stop this madness is through love. That's a simple sentiment, but I believe it at my core."[53]

Native/Environmental

Indigo Girls have become strong advocates for native and indigenous people's rights, particularly as it relates to environmentalism and energy policy. On the surface of it these issues do not seem to affect them directly; although many of the concerns have become even more prescient as climate change continues to intensify. Indeed, they have expressed a great deal of concern, in writing and in song, about both environmental causes and indigenous people. Along with Winona LaDuke (a member of the Ojibwe nation), they co-founded Honor the Earth, a native-led organization committed to indigenous environmental action. The organization "started as a conversation between Amy and Winona at an Earth Day concert in 1991 . . . the people

52. Wiser, "Emily Saliers."
53. Indigo Girls, "Biography—Despite Our Differences."

who were on the front lines of those environmental battles changed us [Emily speaking] forever with their determination, their simple approach to protecting land, water, and air, and their ability to affect change for the sake of all of us."[54] Since 1993, Honor the Earth has addressed "the two primary needs of the Native environmental movement: the need to break the geographic and political isolation of Native communities and the need to increase financial resources for organizing and change."[55] The Indigo Girls have toured in support of this organization, and they continue to inform their fans through email correspondence and website postings.

The way that both Amy and Emily discuss environmental and indigenous activism, through Honor the Earth, also reveals their commitments to address political inequities and oppression. Reflecting on the 1995 Honor the Earth tour, Amy notes: "While monolithic forces like power, mining companies, government atrocities and mismanagement have been a tremendous burden on Indian peoples, time and time again we witnessed how small but organized groups of indigenous activists were speaking truth to power and winning battles."[56] The work with Honor the Earth is intimately related to their wider environmental concerns. In 2003, Amy wrote in an email to their fans:

> It's a very hard time for environmental activism, but I trust our audience sees the connections. We have to move away from our dependence on non–renewable energy resources. The current energy paradigm seems to demand a military

54. Saliers, *A Year a Month*.

55. Honor the Earth, "About Us."

56. Ray, *A Year a Month*.

dominance over the world . . . The laws we
have set up to protect the earth and to protect
our communities are being gutted by the Bush
Administration. . . . But our good intentions certainly do have an agenda and that agenda is oil.
. . . We have abandoned the world community.[57]

Though the issue of environmentalism as it relates to
native peoples does not seem to directly affect either Amy
or Emily, Emily has remarked on how the matter truly does
feel personal: "It's hard to separate [the different issues]
. . . I'm reading about these native communities and about
personal lives and ways of life that are being so negatively
impacted. It feels just as personal to me as anything else in
my life. So I think our environmentalism with respect to
native activism is probably our primary focus."[58] In fact,
a closer examination reveals how much of their activism
and the causes to which they devote so much of themselves
stem from indigenous and environmental work. In addition to advocacy and education work through Honor the
Earth, they have taken initiative to affect environmental
change: "We run our bus on biodiesel and we have all
kinds of things on the rider specifying environmentally
friendly products and requirements, we recycle everything
locally, we do everything we can to make it as green a tour
as possible."[59] Their environmental concerns are, of course,
not limited to their connections to indigenous peoples.
They express concern about potential global oil crises,
particularly in light of oil spills in the Gulf Coast. In June
2010, before the Deepwater Horizon oil spill, which lasted
for three months, was finally contained, Emily wrote,

57. Ray, "April 8, 2003."
58. Schulz, "Let It Be Me."
59. Moss, "Emily Saliers."

"As oil spews into the Gulf of Mexico, in the worst fossil-fueled environmental disaster of our nation's history, we are experiencing a stain on our collective souls. Our fossil fuel-run energy paradigm is not sustainable, and we are literally killing ourselves over it."[60] Both clearly feel a moral responsibility for environmental issues and issues related to solidarity with and freedom for indigenous nations. They have found their niche in the intersection between these two concerns. In fact, they both describe the intricately interwoven strands of all their activism—bound up with indigenous peoples and native justice. Amy, in particular, reflects that learning from native activists resulted in a "lightbulb" moment: "Every bit of activism I do now, in everything from queer rights to immigration issues, is based on a model I learned in Indian Country. The wonder and awe I felt about this experience is beyond measure."[61] Emily echoes this commitment: "supporting these [indigenous] ways of being in relationship with the earth is not a 'co-opting' of a romanticized version of 'Indian Ways.' Rather, the work, sprung from a paradigm of interconnectedness, is practical, respectful, and applicable to all environmental issues."[62] They are careful to tread lightly as white people, cautious not to veer into colonialism and cooptation in their work and their words.

The Indigo Girls, of course, tackle subjects related to indigenous peoples and immigration in their music. One of their most popular songs, "Shame on You," from 1997's *Shaming of the Sun,* celebrates indigenous cultures and addresses immigration issues. The song is upbeat and festive in tone; it tells the story of the singer and her friends,

60. Saliers, "Note . . . June 16, 2010."

61. Ray, *A Year a Month.*

62. Saliers, *A Year a Month.*

whom we understand are nonwhite, perhaps Latino, perhaps native American, or some combination of these groups. It begins explaining that her friends "wash the windows," perhaps illustrating the type of work persons of these groups often must do. Then we get the first explicit mention of race in the song: "I go down to Chicano city park cause it makes me feel so fine . . . The white folks like to pretend it's not [there] but their music's in the air you can hear them singing la la la shame on you You can feel them dancing . . . "

There is a clear division in the town not only between labor, as alluded to in the first lines, but in space; the Chicanos have a separate park that for part of the year remains hidden behind the greenery, making it easier for the "white folk" to ignore their presence. The end of the song brings into even clearer focus the political discrimination at the heart of the song, in one of their most iconic lyrics:

> Let's go road block trippin in the middle of the night up in Gainesville town There'll be blue lights flashin down the long dirt road when they ask me to step out They say we been looking for illegal immigrants can we check your car I say you know it's funny I think we were on the same boat back in 1694.

When asked what song of Amy's Emily wishes she had written, Emily answers "Shame on You," as she "never gets tired of that song. . . . The line 'on the same boat,' that line slays me every single time . . . it always stabs me in the heart in the best way."[63] Through "Shame on You," the Indigo Girls make a political statement about the heightened tension between (mostly) white Americans and immigrants, particularly those labeled "illegal" and "alien."

63. Tongson, "Emily Saliers."

The song illustrates that "white folk" cannot actually claim the title "native," if we trace American history beyond the nation's founding. The song's title "Shame On You" begins as a lively statement against sadness, and moves to a more pointed political critique of discriminating against people groups: those in power decide who belongs and who does not by staking out arbitrary boundaries lines of legal and illegal.

From the same album, "Scooter Boys" also addresses indigenous people, a song that Emily calls "a fierce commentary on colonialism."[64] It offers a meditation on history of injustice against native people, particularly those in South and Central America:

> Scooter boys and Argentineans Europe shed the blood of the Indian Here I sit in the land of plenty . . . You're just another colonial terrorist . . . Way down south where the Maya reign Zapata reading poetry in his grave They said we're stealing from the best to feed the poor Well they need it more.

"Scooter Boys" juxtaposes righteous indignation and a feeling of impotence in the face of injustice and violence. It tells the story of a patterned history of violent colonization and pillaging native groups—Indians, Mayans, Zapatistas—to provide for others. Native American (inclusive of north, central, and south) justice issues are clearly of central importance to the Indigo Girls. Both have spent time traveling and working among groups in Cuba and Chiapas; Amy feels a particular draw toward the Zapatista cause in Mexico. Although the group has spent their existence fighting land wars and struggling for political acceptance, she writes that they demonstrate to her

64. Saliers, *A Year a Month.*

hope: "Hope is symbolized by people in my community who have seen the worst but persevere and remain active participants. . . . When I visit the Zapatistas in the jungle and they've built schools and communities—people who have suffered but rise above it and still love each other and love people."[65] This song, however, does not reverberate with hope; it begins in a place of critique, reflecting the Indigo Girls' perspective on colonization, which motivates them to find solidarity with indigenous people groups and advocate on behalf of them.

Environmental issues emerge in more subtle ways too. There are examples of songs from their catalog that utilize nature-imagery as guiding metaphors, some of which have already been discussed ("World Falls," "The Wood Song"). These songs often blend the natural world with whatever else is operative in the lyrics. Other songs focus on the natural environment, in a sense romanticizing it, like the short and percussion-driven, "Bitterroot," from 2002's *Become You*. Using the national park in southwestern Montana of the same name as the backdrop, the song repeats the lines:

> Tonight I'll be sleeping on the mountain top,
> I've got a billion stars for my witness
> In the morning I'll go down and the sun comes up,
> I'll take a drink from the Bitterroot River.

In between this chorus are call-and-answer phrases. The first asks: "Have you been lonely?" with the answer, "Yes I've been lonely." And the initial voice responds: "I've been lonely too." The second time the word "travelin'" replaces with word "lonely." Given the opening lines that repeat throughout the song, we are not given an indication that the singer is accompanied by another person. The simple

65. Kinkaid, "Indigo Girls."

and joyful song is about communing with nature and finding solace and solidarity with the mountain, stars, sun, and river. It is joyful and it is peaceful.

The song "Cedar Tree" from 1992's *Rites of Passage,* is fairly short on words, but uses nature imagery to symbolize strength and redemption: "you dug a well you dug it deep for every wife you buried you planted a cedar tree . . . I dig a well I dig it deep and for my only love I plant a cedar tree." The song is about memory, remembering those dead and gone. The cedar tree is a living symbol for a memory. Biblically speaking, the cedar tree is a symbol of strength, so the tree could be interpreted as a symbol of hope for redemption and strength in honor, as well as memory, of those who have died.

The song "John," the second track on *Beauty Queen Sister,* tells the story of John, with whom the singer has a familial relationship, perhaps like a mentor. The lyrics tell that John's "family's from these parts / Before the white men got there," indicating Native American roots. The singer describes herself as "the girl from the city," and describes the patience and kindness that John shows her: "John's work is never done / Helping the girl out from the big city." There is a certain nostalgia and romance to the way the song describes John's relationship with the environment and the land, specifically noting the simplicity of his subsistence: he "knows that he could make a killing / Selling rights to fish the trout / to rich city men who come in," but that does not appeal to him. He is content to live life consistent with the respect of his ancestors, and the singer expresses her depth of gratitude for the way that "he kindly tolerates / The wanderer in" her.

Queer

As previously noted, both Emily and Amy are openly gay, and therefore issues surrounding sexuality and queerness have been a part of their message throughout their career. Their discussion of issues surrounding sexuality extends into politics, the music business, and gender issues in general. Because they are women, issues of sexism are also wrapped up in their addressing sexuality and gender. Taking on issues of sexuality in their activism did not come naturally or comfortably at first, but once they realized the power and responsibility accompanying their public roles as musicians, and the expectations from their growing audiences, speaking out for LGBTQ+ human rights became part of the fabric of what it meant to be an Indigo Girl. In 1993 they were invited to DC to play for the Pride March, which was also covered on MTV. There were 800,000 to 1 million people gathered at the National Mall in Washington, both to celebrate queer identities and to demand full protection under the law and equal rights. Participating in this event proved pivotal for both Emily and Amy. In reflecting on what that day meant, Amy notes that the day was a "triumph": "not just a day to be active on a large community level, but just as importantly to affirm each other's singular love relationships in a world where they were rarely recognized as legitimate."[66] Emily notes with humility, "To stand in solidarity with hundreds of thousands of people, queers and straight allies, is a moment in time I carry with me for the rest of my life. . . . Music was our voice for inclusion."

In 1998 they set out to play a "high school tour," around the South with the goal to "play some songs for the

66. Ray, *A Year a Month.*

students and do a sort of a 'career' day where they could ask questions and we could talk about music."[67] The impetus came as they observed arts education funding shrinking; they wanted to be a voice for the arts for students. During their first show, Amy—somewhat accidentally—sang the original lyric in "Shame On You": "I keep fucking up." Later, they received a call that the rest of the shows had been canceled because of this slip up; however, as Emily tells it, "The real reason behind the cancellations became immediately clear: Amy and I were lesbians."[68] The backlash and accompanying vitriol was not shocking to either of them, but it *was* painful nonetheless. What they were not prepared for was the response from the students who staged their own counter-protests. Emily remembers: "Even the ACLU became involved to protect their rights. In the truest sense of the word, the activism of those students was *awesome*. They spoke truth to power, they inspired Amy and me, they brought issues of injustice towards gays to the light, and they exercised their rights as citizens."[69]

Another profound decisive moment in their queer activism took place in 2007 when they participated in the True Colors Tour organized by Cyndi Lauper. The tour had several overlapping purposes, perhaps most significantly to advocate for the passage of the Matthew Shepard Act, which would expand the 1969 federal Hate Crimes Act to include crimes against someone where gender or sexuality was the target. In 2009 Obama signed the Matthew Shepard Act into law. Seeing this kind of progress, Emily reflects: "This kind of activism through music is the

---

67. Saliers, *A Year a Month*.

68. Saliers, *A Year a Month*.

69. Saliers, *A Year a Month*.

heart and soul of what Amy and I love best."[70] Their music, identities, and activism cannot be separated or compartmentalized: "Activism changes lives for the better. The music we bring along lifts our spirits through the arduous work for change."[71]

Not surprisingly, several of their songs incorporate issues related to sexuality, gay rights, and gender issues. "Philosophy of Loss," from *Come on Now Social,* takes head-on the issue of homosexuality and the Christian church. Emily remarks that the song addresses "how the church deals with gays and so on," stating that the issues are "political, but they're also very personal to me, and that comes out in the song."[72] The lyrics waste no words to get to the heart of the matter, explaining, "Welcome to why the church has died / . . . / And marries itself to the state."

Throughout the Bible the theme of exile indentifies God's people—sometimes the people were placed into exile by enemies of God and against God's will; other times Scripture depicts the exile as part of God's punishment for injustice, oppression, or other evildoing. In "Philosophy of Loss," exile is used to differentiate the singers from those religious voices; in a sense the religious elite, the church, has placed them in exile. The kingdom here is not the kingdom of God (the common language in the Bible to explain God's reign of peace, justice, and goodness), but the kingdom of hate. The song continues to explain the experience of the exiled: "Everyone is free / And the doors open wide to all straight men & women / But they are not open to me." Here the song indicts a church that has institutionalized homophobia and violence. Juxtaposing them in the

70. Saliers, *A Year a Month.*

71. Saliers, *A Year a Month.*

72. Schulz, "Let It Be Me."

same critique marries them as part of the same system of sin. It also surmises that a significant piece of the problem in the American context is the "marriage" of the church to the state, systems in which the state has granted political power to the church. As the critique about political abuse of power persists, they continue to ask the questions beginning with "who is teaching kids to . . .", suggesting that all these unjust practices and systems are taught, not a given, and therefore the kids must also be taught otherwise. They insist that "There are a few who would be true out of love / And love is hard." Central to the Indigo Girls' theology and witness is the centrality of love, and often when systems and structures deserve critique it is because love as a driving force is missing. The song ends with a glimmer of hope, asking: "Who is teaching kids to be leaders / and the way that it is meant to be?" This song was released in 1999, a year after their High School Tour. Perhaps it offers a reflection on their experience in and rejection by these communities, particularly the adults.

The external struggles as members of the greater queer community, as well as political and social struggles for equality, give Emily and Amy a clear personal stake in the matter. One of the initial ways this became a personal struggle for the two was in their musical career. Both have been "out" since the genesis of their musical career, and their sexuality certainly played a role in the perceived validity of their songwriting. In large part, being part of a music community gave them a greater sense of identity; Amy relates that after she moved back to Atlanta to attend Emory, "I . . . found a music scene . . . It was a scene I could be a part of. I met a lot of older women—not all of them were gay, but they were strong women. Music became my whole identity—not my sexuality."[73] However, as a band, they certainly encountered significant critique and prejudice because their sexuality placed them outside the mainstream. They have remarked consistently about the difficulty for women in general in the music business, and that is significantly magnified if the female's sexuality is also seen as contradicting the "norm."

The Indigo Girls participated as one of the headlining acts during the initial iteration of Lilith Fair (1997–1999), a touring music festival founded by Sarah McLachlan as "a celebration of women in music"[74]—an experience that highlighted some of their struggle, yet also validated their place in the music industry. Amy and Emily saw their participation in this summer event as vital because they believed in the importance of recognizing "women's growing role and visibility in the music business."[75] Although Lilith Fair remains "one of the highest grossing touring festivals in the world," Emily recalls, "there were naysayers, and, you know, there is no way women can sell this many tickets. There was a lot of sexism in the industry at the time. Lilith held this joyous 'yes we can' feeling and it was a great tour."[76] Participation in Lilith Fair—for three years—stands out for them in large part because of the fertile ground it was for kinship and collaboration with other women artists. Yet, it did not come without struggle. Amy remembers: "we felt like it'd be crazy not to collaborate when we were amongst so many other musicians traveling together and sharing the stage. At first we met some resistance, and I think being queer was not too cool at the time, I honestly

---

73. Robertson, "Rockin' Out."

74. Fair, "About."

75. Indigo Girls, "1999: Come On Now Social Biography."

76. Ragogna, "Brilliant Dreams."

think there was some fear inside some musicians that the association with us would be damaging."[77] Not only have they had to fight discrimination in the music industry as females, but they have had amplified detractions because they are women and gay.

Their struggle during the mid-late nineties was not without impact. Brandi Carlile was coming of age, and coming to terms with her own queer sexuality, while trying to pursue a music career of her own. She is now a five-time Grammy winner, with incredible commercial success. In her memoir, *Broken Horses,* she credits the Indigo Girls, in particular their participation in Lilith Fair, with shaping her own identity as musician and helping her embrace her own unique personhood as a queer singer-songwriter. In her reflection, she writes:

> [The Indigo Girls] had androgynous music and images. They were singing love songs and using same-gender pronouns. That should have felt normal, but to me it was radical. I felt like I knew them . . . and I couldn't understand why. Whatever it was, it was in their voices. They sounded like they were resisting something . . . and I couldn't make sense of it at the time, but I knew that somehow I was in that fight too.[78]

In 2018, Brandi had the opportunity to honor the influence of both the Indigo Girls and Lilith Fair when she organized her own festival featuring an all-female lineup. About it, she remarks, "My festival, Girls Just Wanna Weekend . . . It really reminded me of Lilith Fair. Everyone there knew it

77. Ray, *A Year a Month.*

78. Carlile, *Broken Horses,* 62.

was something special . . . The Indigo Girls were there, too, which made it feel even more full circle."[79]

As much as a triumph as the years of Lilith Fair were, Amy and Emily continued to face criticism. In 2002, in response to a piece by David Hadju in the *New York Magazine,* Amy wrote an essay titled "Queer and Fucked." The original essay claims that lesbians limit "the growth of folk music, [and] are also damning it with mediocrity," to which Ray responds, "gay musicians suffer more, because as far as the mainstream rock media is concerned, our image is our handicap."[80] She reflects, "It's never really a good time in the mainstream music industry to be a queer girl with a guitar. I can look at the trajectory of my own career and see that the more political the Indigo Girls have become, the less radio play and press we have received." She continues, "Being a woman, being a gay woman is socially very different from being a straight man. There has been a need for people of second or third class social statuses to create separate spaces for community and expression."[81] She continues to levy her critique, largely aimed at media:

> Maybe the movement for acceptance is making some progress on the street level, but it's not being reflected by the media. We are still distilled down to the demographic of our audience and the particulars of our sex lives. Our music is not written about positively or for the inherent worth of the music, our progress as songwriters is never noted, and we just aren't taken seriously as artists.[82]

79. Carlile, *Broken Horses,* 230.
80. Ray, "Queer and Fucked."
81. Ray, "Queer and Fucked."
82. Ray, "Queer and Fucked."

A bit of an overstatement, considering the Indigo Girls are considerably popular, however, these thoughts from Amy give insight into the struggles she and Emily have faced throughout their musical career because of both their gender and their sexuality. This highlights the duality persistent in their career—they have experienced sustained success, and yet they still fight being too narrowly defined by their sexuality.

Amy's and Emily's deep convictions about the power and necessity for a life well-lived, and for genuine social and political change also drives much of the content in their songs related to sexuality and gay rights. Emily often repeats her belief that love is what is missing in public discourse, domestic and international policy, as well as mundane human interaction; love is the only thing that will genuinely change things. Another song from *Despite Our Differences*, "I Believe in Love," is "a gorgeous folk-soul lullaby, and proves this point with its message of tolerance and the necessity of understanding 'despite our differences.'"[83] The song itself is a love song, proclaiming, "I still believe despite our differences that what we have's enough / And I believe in you and I believe in love." The song is broad in scope; it does not address particulars about what constitutes an "appropriate" relationship, in terms of gender, but rather offers a testament to struggle in relationship and the commitment to remaining with someone because of love, despite the reality that someone could get hurt. However, the song is about more than love; the title of the album, *Despite Our Differences*, comes from the chorus of the song, and represents a depth of love that transcends one-on-one relationship. The line of the song is meant to illustrate: "in a global context how we can, despite our differences

83. Ray, "Queer."

as peoples, or cultures, or countries, or whatever it is, we can co-exist without destroying each other. So that's the hope and that's the belief."[84] Therefore, although the song does not explicitly address sexuality or gay rights, it fits at this point in the conversation because of its interpretation of love and the power of love to transcend differences, from the differences between two people to broad global, cultural differences.

Another song from the same album addresses, still somewhat abstractly, the difficulties those outside the "mainstream" face in the music industry. "Rock and Roll Heaven's Gate" begins with the proclamation: "no one wants to hear the truth, / coming from three political queers."[85] As previously discussed, the Indigo Girls have felt consistent pushback from the mainstream music industry because they do not fit into a neat "market-friendly" category. This song speaks to that experience, and the subsequent freedom they have felt by *not* fitting into expectations of the media or the mangers: "Free to be a loser / . . . / Free to be a trend / . . . / Free to be a backlash over and over again." Even though they have felt discrimination and even neglect because of their image, they have remained free from conformity, and they have maintained the ability to be true to themselves. Amy notes that this song, along with "Money Made You Mean" (discussed above), "were comments on the greed and absurdity of the music industry."[86]

The song also speaks to potential audiences who have been numbed or dumbed-down by the conformity of the mainstream, Top-40 music industry; they perhaps

84. Wiser, "Emily Saliers."

85. The "three" includes Ray and Saliers, and singer Pink, who collaborated with them for this song.

86. Ray, *A Year a Month*.

speak for these audiences with the lines: "You say, 'I'm losing inspiration, / one band at a time. / I gotta know there's someone, somewhere, out there singing for our side.'" Again, even though they do not explicitly name "our side," we can connect the dots to understand this as being artists outside the industry's standards of conformity, which for the Indigo Girls, relates directly to their sexuality. They further address this struggle using the biblical eschatological symbol of "crossing over," leaving an element of hope that there will be an eventual shift in the landscape, even if it is in the metaphorical "afterlife" (applying the symbol here to their music careers and the music industry)—the "Rock and Roll Heaven's Gate."

"They Won't Have Me," the twelfth track on *Despite Our Differences,* relates the existential feeling of isolation resulting from being "different." The song begins with the line: "They won't have me, but I love this place." There is a sense of simultaneously being at home and being alienated from where (or what) one belongs. The chorus sings: "All this love to offer, all this love to waste," which could be interpreted from the perspective of the Indigo Girls' sexual identity as being *able* to love, but not being *allowed* to love because of political and social contexts and systems that explicitly or implicitly outlaw and alienate homosexuality. Though the song is implicit in all of this, perhaps the clearest nod to what is meant is in the following lines: "Now you know what divides us / Is just a difference someone made." Here the theme of *difference* on the album emerges, which is quite possibly sexuality at its core; sexual identity is a human-created division. It is a rather melancholy song, somewhat lacking in the hope of previous songs, but still centered on love as the most crucial thing, "despite our differences." Amy often jokes—tinged with no small hint of seriousness—about her decision to live in a small town in rural north Georgia, an area not exactly known for the progressive politics of urban Atlanta: "I like to live in an area where no one likes me . . . there are really good people enmeshed in this society and this is how you make change, by having conversations with one person at a time."[87]

One of their earlier songs, "Trouble," from the 1999 album *Come on Now Social*, offers one of the most explicit songs addressing sexuality. The song begins addressing all forms of "trouble," putting it in the geographic context particular to the Indigo Girls: "Trouble came around here / Here in the South we fix it something to eat." The song then delves into different forms of "trouble," using the words "strangers" and "aliens" to set up the context that follows, thus linking "trouble" with things that do not belong, or perhaps people that do not fit. We then hear a combination of images that fit, for the Indigo Girls, into this understanding of "trouble," including the lines: "I pledge my allegiance to the dollar / And when the clergy take a vote all the gays will pay again / Cause there's more than one kind of criminal white collar." Focused on the role that clergy and the institutional church have played in maintaining power at the expense of queer individuals' inclusion, they denounce the trouble they observe by turning others' rhetoric around to illustrate its illegitimacy or illogical nature.

The song wonders how God could be blamed for natural disasters (as we heard following Hurricane Katrina in 2005, or the 2010 earthquake in Haiti); and they further critique industries that potentially poison the water that flows into poor populations. These lines also include a renouncement of capitalist consumer culture, in which we

87. Ray, "Optimism."

pledge allegiance, not to the American flag, but "to the dollar," or perhaps even more stringent, to clergy who pledge allegiance to power gained through political cooperation vis-à-vis American capitalism. To be sure, the song offers an explicit critique of anti-gay discrimination by saying that clergy vote on definitions of sin, suggesting that homosexuality is not necessarily antithetical to religion, but decisions by those in power have declared it sinful. They go on to imagine a future in which some of this "trouble" will be resolved: "One day the war will stop & we'll grow a peaceful crop / And a girl can get a wife & we can bring you back to life." However, we get the sense that the heart of the problem will not be resolved, as they claim we will "be no closer to the understanding." Even if the trouble is gone, that does not solve the central problems of misunderstanding and lack of communication and empathy. The song does take head-on the issue of homosexuality, and clearly illustrates that as a source of "trouble" in our society, but perhaps not for the reasons many think, in fact it is trouble *because* of the perspective that there is a reason for "gays [to] pay again."

On their 2009 full-length, *Poseidon and the Bitter Bug,* the song "Love of Our Lives," offers a message of hope and solidarity, again with love at the center of the message of transformation. The title emerges in the chorus: "We've been fighting for the love of our lives." The song mainly addresses the repeating theme of the Indigo Girls' music of the persistence of life, in spite of struggle, difference, or potential pain: "All around us things come apart. / Broken pieces. Broken hearts, / Fix me, oil me, match me with the next best thing." It relates to the desperation one feels at the prospect of losing the person one loves: "I beg you don't go.

/ . . . / I am fighting for the love of my life." The fight here is for a relationship on the brink of ending.

We do get a sense that there is something deeper at work in the struggle of the song, perhaps a more abstract principle, hinted at in the lines: "Person to person, nation to nation / Heels dug in no communication. / While the time speaks of weathering." These lines give heed to a more universal struggle, one that must be worn down along the test of time. Emily has remarked, as quoted above, and I repeat here: "In time, the evolution of gay rights, for lack of a better term, will make us look back and wonder why there was such hatred and homophobia. But I sincerely doubt we will get to that point of understanding during my lifetime."[88] She repeats this sentiment later, around the time the album came out, following the defeat of California's Proposition 8: "Prop 8 was a huge disappointment, a huge setback. I still can't believe how far behind we are in the evolution of human rights in terms of gay people."[89] With this perspective in the background of our hearing this song, we should notice greater purpose and meaning to the words "fighting for the love of our lives." Additionally, the plural pronoun communicates a collective endeavor, a struggle for collective rights and/or freedom to love. This is more than a grasping to save one relationship, but a fight for love—any love—that exists outside heteronormativity.

One of their newest songs, "Country Radio," from 2020's *Look Long*, addresses the tension both Amy and Emily felt growing up gay in the South. Emily wrote the song, noting that she loved Country music growing up, but she "couldn't fit [her] personal life in the life of people

88. Saliers, "Emily's Answers."

89. Moss, "Saliers." Proposition 8 was a piece of legislation defeated in the November 2008 elections in California. If it had passed, it would have amended California's constitution to allow gay marriages.

who wrote the songs" she loved on the radio. The chorus of "Country Radio" laments, "I wanna be that boy, I wanna be that girl / I wanna know what it's like to fall in love like / Most of the rest of the world / . . . / I'm just a gay kid in a small town / Who loves country radio." The song takes on the theme of *otherness*. Emily notes that the song, while about her personal experience, is for "Anyone who's felt other by society, church," and this experience "is common and if you've never felt it, you're out of touch with what's going on in your life."[90] *Otherness* as a theme emerges in both Amy's and Emily's lyrics and the way they talk about their vocation as artists. During a 2017 conference, Ray noted that the feeling otherness was something that developed, and she has always worked to "use this to make something good"; it was her experience of being *other*—in all the intersectionality of her identity that helped her develop empathy and compassion.

Independent Media and Music Community

As previously noted, Amy's own record label was a project borne of her own desire to hear more the kind of music she enjoyed. Emily calls music the "great galvanizer," and insists that it only matters in community. Amy furthers this idea by saying: "Emily and I . . . think that you gather people together in a space and try to break down the barriers by having people focus on the act of listening and act of being together and forgetting all the things that divide us . . . that's a catalyst for change because it challenges and emboldens you."[91] In their lengthy retrospective blog, *A Month a Year*, stories of how different albums and songs

90. Jackson, "Indigo Girls on *The Paste Happiest Hour*."
91. Ray, "Optimism."

came together often center on the collaborations that took place—in the writing, producing, and playing together. Although they acknowledge the myriad benefits of having the backing of major labels, especially early in their career, they have expressed both relief and comfort "returning" to their independent roots. After being with Epic Records, and then, briefly, Hollywood Records, in 2008 they established their own label, IG Recordings, and, as Emily describes, "It was liberating . . . we could pick our own release date, schedule our own artwork deadlines, spend the money absolutely prudently, and not have to think about pleasing anyone but ourselves."[92]

Voter Education/American Political System

Of course, many of their songs can be understood to critique the US political system implicitly—because of their explicit take on indigenous rights, peace, and queerness— and we have already seen these themes in both "Tether" and "The Rise of the Black Messiah." There are also several songs that more directly take on domestic electoral politics. "Able to Sing," from *Beauty Queen Sister,* uses patriotic imagery and spins the meanings of those images. For example, "Oh, was a blind force trauma from the fireworks / That someone is celebrating while another gets hurt," takes the generally celebratory fireworks and notes that the underbelly of the celebration hides the hurt caused to another. Further, "While the rocket's red glare / Gives proof through the night / If some thing's not right," alludes to the US national anthem, but again, turning the words on their head.

92. Saliers, *A Year a Month.*

The opening lines of "Change My Heart," from *Look Long,* uses scientific parallels to take on the division and factions that characterize American politics and society: "The four fundamental forces came to play / In the American schism." The song turns inward recognizing that the divisions can be healed in small part, and starting with the individual: "Change my heart / . . . / Change my mind when I think I understand things I can't." This plea sounds like a prayer; maybe it is *us* who need to change as much as external structures do.

Finally, the title track from *Look Long* takes on the unsettled and chaotic zeitgeist in twenty-first-century United States. The song challenges the listener to take the long view, illustrated in the repetition of the title. Emily observes, "people feel lost in these political times." She wrote the song to allow the audience to "lament our limitations," and to "look beyond what's right in front of us, take the long view of things, and strive to do better." She notes that the lyrics hail "an all but vanished form of American identity": the "Apollo Mission glasses / etched in red, white, and blue commemoration," belonged to her "Nixon Republican" grandmother. Reflecting the lost-ness of the current state of democracy, the lyrics protest: "I'm no AWOL patriot because I've dodged your party lines / I will always love my troubled nation this beautiful land." The song "is both a lament and a prayer of hope for the country she loves."[93] The final verse is a reminder: "Because these aren't the best of times and they're not the worst / Just like the edge of Earth is an illusion," as well as a call to put aside our "short-sighted plans" and to "Look long." A clear invective against despair, the song is a reminder

---

93. Indigo Girls, "On Their 16th Studio Album."

of the great "arc of history," to borrow from Dr. King, that bends towards justice.

Georgia and the South

Included in the "Activism" section of their website are resources and links to organizations working specifically for justice issues in Georgia and around the South. Many musicians, in order to gain both audience and industry recognition, find they must relocate to more music-centric locations: Los Angeles, New York, Nashville, or Seattle. From the beginning of their careers, both Amy and Emily committed themselves to being home at least every three-to-four weeks, "home" being Georgia. More specifically, Emily has remained in the Atlanta metro area, and Amy has been in rural north-central Georgia for most of the last 30 years. Therefore, although many of their songs that mention the South are not overtly *activist* in tone or content, it is fitting to include them here. The ideas of *place* as representing both comforts of home and the struggle with belonging in this place called home emerge throughout their catalog. In many ways the South often represents the fraught intersectionality of both Amy's and Emily's identities: they are both white, which places them in positions of privilege, yet being queer in the South casts them as outsiders. Throughout their career, we hear them wrestle with the dueling privilege and oppression layered with the realities of calling a place home that often rejects much of their identity.

"Southland in the Springtime," from 1990's *Nomads Indians Saints,* offers a love song to the natural world, in their home context of the South. In *Watershed* Emily talks about writing this song, after their first major label album.

Following months on tour, away from home, and living out of suitcases, buses, and to-go meals, her response, which often happens for musicians after their first period of intensive recording and touring, was to write about the longing for home. Specifically, the song "chronicles . . . the route" they would tour across the South—from Atlanta, to New Orleans, to Austin, and back. This song reflects that longing for home in the environment of a Southern Spring: "there's something 'bout the Southland in the springtime / Where the waters flow with confidence and reason." The images of the Southland that she longs for center on the scents and sounds, not least of which include the natural surroundings. The homesick theme of the song does include people and food, like "cider" and "boiled peanuts," but the song remains primarily a love-song to a favorite season in the South, marked by images of landscape and nature.

A song from several years later, off 2009's *Poseidon and the Bitter Bug*, "Salty South" briefly touches on land struggles in the United States. In this song ,the South, their home, is context for their critique once again. The song begins as the singer is sitting with an older man who will tell her stories of the South, history that long outlives him. We get a sense of her own perspective on the history, more specifically these stories that likely go untold:

> Drain that land
> For a better plan
> Sugarcane and the civil man
> But now the ringin' dead them pines
> Planted in that time
> We gonna keep on killin' till they get it right.

The upsetting history of raping the land and killing the people who were native to the South (specifically) is juxtaposed with the romanticized re-telling of the South's history. While the older generations tell these stories, the unseemly history is revealed: gritty, underneath layers of buried nostalgia. In songs like "Salty South," we see issues of place and geography, of land ownership and history, centuries-old struggles for ideology and justice in concert.

The title track to the 2002 album, *Become You,* also tackles this Southern-based burden of history, tied particularly to the land. This song confronts the struggle of the Southerner facing her land's own troubled history and wanting to distance herself from the injustices of the past: "Our Southern blood, my heresy, damn that ol' confederacy." The song also offers an apology to those who have been (and continue to be) victim to the South's history: "I'm sorry for what you have learned, / . . . / All your daddies fought in vain, leave you with the mark of Cain." The song nods to the legacy of the Confederacy: folks caught between defending their ancestors, but rebuking the cause for which they fought; the latter often falling victim to the former. We get a sense of the ways that the "sins of the fathers," so to speak, affect the sons and daughters for generations. The mark of Cain is a biblical reference to Genesis 4, when Cain kills his brother Abel (the mythological first murder), and receives this curse from God: "Listen; your brother's blood is crying out to me from the ground! And now you are cursed from the ground, which has opened its mouth to receive your brother's blood from your hand."[94] Despite Cain's protestations, God continues to "put a mark on Cain, so that no one who came upon him would kill him."[95] Therefore, the punishment for the murderer is that he must continue to suffer the curse his own sin brought

94. Gen 4:10b–11.
95. Gen 4:15b.

upon him. By calling upon this biblical symbol, "Become You," illustrates the sin of the white colonizers and slave-holders who killed their own brothers—literally during the Civil War, and metaphorically in the slaughter of Natives and African slaves. The resulting curse was that the blood continues to cry out in the Southern land, and future generations continue to feel the effects of this tainted history. These effects are demonstrated in the following verse:

> The center holds, so they say.
> . . . The center held the bonded slave
> for the sake of industry.
> The center held the bloody hand
> of the executioner man.

The "center," the *status quo*, represents those in authority or in power who determine the norms or policies. They have used and continue to use those things as an excuse to perpetrate violence, discrimination, and dehumanization; for the sake of profit and industry, those in power excused execution, torture, and lynching in the system of slavery.

The opening song from *Look Long*, wrestles with the identity and legacy of being gay and Southern. Amy Ray wrote "Shit Kickin'" and notes that it is about "your legacy growing around you like kudzu."[96] To be sure, the song refers to "That kudzu covered me / Like it would set me free," using the ubiquitous "America's favorite weed,"[97] to juxtapose the image of a plant known for its invasive and smothering quality, and the thought of that setting someone free. As the Girls' website describes, the song is "both a love letter to her Southern heritage and a refusal to be complacent about the region's legacy of prejudice and racism," revealed in lyrics like: "Damn that trickery / it got

96. Masters, "Amy Ray."
97. Finch, "Kudzu."

111

the best of me, I'm gonna / Tear it down and start again." Outsiders might question both Amy's and Emily's decision to stay rooted in Georgia given its fraught history. For both of them, it is a commitment to work to redeem a place they love *despite* its blemished past, and a recognition that healing cannot happen from the outside. Emily once remarked: "The South gets a bad rap for being backwards, but we're at the heart—we're at the center of the fight. Out of those ashes rise the true heroes."[98] Ultimately, they both operate out of the conviction that to witness deep and lasting change anywhere, the South specifically, means they must be committed to be part of the work, not merely critique as ex-pat observers. Amy sums this belief up: "we think that you gather people together in a space and try to break down the barriers by having people focus on the act of listening and act of being together and forgetting all the things that divide us . . . that's a catalyst for change because it challenges and emboldens you."[99] They have committed themselves in word and deed, including where they choose to invest and put down roots, to activism and seeing the work through.

98. HeadCount, "Emily Saliers."
99. Ray, "Optimism."

4

"Let It Be Me"

Imagination—Hope and Freedom

Ultimately, all of the advocacy and activism, the issues towards which Amy and Emily have worked, have roots in their shared belief in justice, freedom, equality, and love. They remain driven by love, demonstrated in their public work towards political and social issues. Because of their core understanding of the equality of human beings—often phrased in terms of the "human family"—and the necessity for equality in all forms, they find themselves advocating on behalf of people like themselves (i.e., female, homosexual), and those different from them (i.e., immigrants, indigenous people, the impoverished). Their music and activism is tied together by their belief in a solidarity with other human beings, which is itself a theological belief, made more relevant in light of liberation and other "contextual" theologies. Emily reflects on this: "The way in and the way out is through a human being . . .

We have a human need for each other—to find our respite and refuge and rest. There's a codependency."[1]

All of these songs, in substance and style, work toward their desire for justice and truth—freedom from oppression, which they believe music has a unique power to confront. The prophetic content and effect of the Indigo Girls' music reaches beyond critique, however. As previously discussed, their prophetic witness denounces, to be sure, but even more significantly, it proclaims, it imagines what *could be*. This prophetic imagination declares what is possible; it dwells in the future potential of equality, justice, freedom, and peace. The Indigo Girls' music speaks to hope and freedom, and it embraces one's responsibility for bringing about change with and among fellow members of the human family; in doing this, it is deeply prophetic.

One well-known example of their messag of individual responsibilty for enacting transformation can be found in the album *Nomads Indians Saints*. "Hammer and a Nail" is about working to create and reveal something beautiful in what remains. The transformation at the heart of the song is both about the world around the singer and also the inner work of transformation of the singer herself. The beginning of external transformation, the singer stresses, is in the internal awareness of one's own place in the world, and the importance of taking initiative and action—using both one's hands and one's head. To a certain degree, this starting point calls to mind the New Testament words from James: "faith by itself, if it has no works, is dead."[2] There is the implicit idea that philosophizing about change, or believing the world should be a certain way is not enough;

1. Kinkaid, "Indigo Girls."
2. Jas 2:14.

rather, one must take part in working for transformation. The song ends with words that elaborate on these ideas:

> I had a lot of good intentions
> . . . But my life is more than a vision
> The sweetest part is acting after making a decision
> I started seeing the whole as a sum of its parts.
> My life is part of the global life
> . . . A distant nation my community
> A street person my responsibility
> If I have a care in the world I have a gift to bring.

She admits that it is tempting to remain selfish, put in the requisite years at a job, then retire comfortably; it is tempting to give into the debilitating and overwhelming idea that one person cannot affect any change. This sone ang these lines specifically, however, reiterate the theological idea of solidarity throughout the Indigo Girls canon. This idea is phrased in terms of belonging to one another, bearing responsibility for other people, and being but one member of the larger human family. Hence, it is up to each of us as individuals to pool our resources and gifts, and contribute to the work for the change and betterment of those around us—our "community" and our "responsibility."

"Let It Be Me," from *Rites of Passage,* is also about the motivation to take on the work of change, in a sense, echoing the famous quote from Gandhi, to "be the change you wish to see in the world." The change wished for at the core of this song is for peace; the chorus is the most telling in its urging for peaceful transformation: "let it be me (this is not a fighting song) let it be me (not a wrong for a wrong) let it be me, if the world is night shine my life like a light." in its expressed desire to bring light to the world, the song also recalls the children's spiritual "This Little Light of Mine," and Jesus' declaration in the Sermon on the Mount that his disciples "are the light of the world." The opening verse emphasizes the belief in solidarity and connectedness across all kinds of borders: "while the politicians shadowbox the power ring in an endless split decision never solve anything from a neighbor's distant land I heard the strain of the common man." The song acknowledges the despair felt when observing the impotency of politicians who never seem to work for significant change of any sort. However, the singer feels a kinship with all those across the world who echo the same sentiment to "let it be me." The second verse continues the "common humanity" theme and our significant personal responsibility:

> the president has no good idea who the masses
> are well I'm one of them and I'm among friends
> trying to see beyond the fences of our own back-
> yard I've seen the kingdoms blow like ashes in
> the winds of change but the power of truth is
> the fuel for the flame so the darker the ages get
> there's a stronger beacon yet

In addition to these recurring themes, the song criticizes political systems and symbols, as is explicit in claiming the authority figures are out of touch with the "common masses," of which the singer claims to be part. But perhaps the most important (and theological?) message in all of this is the contrast set up between lightness and dark. Here the song calls on the strongest power of truth to reach beyond and shine through the darkness of ignorance, impotence, and lack of political will to change things. The true power of this truth is in the common masses who will rise up with the empowering song to "let it be me."

From the 2004 album, *All that We Let In,* "Perfect World," offers a ringing example of the imaginative quality, instructive in its vision of an alternative world. The song speaks to the potential and promise of each person's role and ability to contribute to changing the world. The opening lines declare, "We get to be a ripple in the water," hinting at the precipice of change, though it is ambiguous as to the resulting impact. Any of these things could serve destructive means, or they could result in positive change. The song carries this message of our positive and negative effects in the world around us. The lines of the chorus speak to our role—both individually and collectively—in shaping the world around us. The "forgetting" and "denying" our part in creating and changing the world around us is detrimental on two levels: we forget that we have great power to destroy and damage the earth, each other, our relationships; and we also forget that we have great power to change the world for the better.

As the song reaches its conclusion, it offers no resolution, and leaves the listener with a plea, phrased as a question: "Can we learn to live another way?" The song urges listeners to deny numbness, the conscious ignorance of turning away from our responsibility for the state of the world, and to embrace the possibility of living another way, leaving us with the reminder that we "get to be a ripple in the water." Emily has used this metaphor to talk about how she perceives her role as a musician; there is a "continuum of gifts given . . . you can't own music, even if you create it." This gift, she insists, "It's not solely mine, I'm just the vehicle for it . . . ripple in the pond, to use the cliché."[3]

The title track to the same album is also visionary in its acceptance of all that has been, declaring "We're better off for all that we let in." "All That We Let In," reminds us of the transforming power of pain and struggle in order to come out stronger and better on the other side. Emily

3. Saliers and Saliers, "Creativity Conversation."

recounts that the song came from a true story of a woman she met who she later learned was killed by a drunk driver. The lyrics lament loss on several levels—of individual lives lost too soon and about "Bush and the Middle East war . . . It was a song of lament and a look at the beauty of both vast and simple things."[4]

The song also speaks to the spiritual angle of struggling in a world accompanied by pain and death, —"we're better off for all that we let in"—and to the common fear of the finality of death—"And the brutal crossing over when it's time." The transition seems too sudden and yet plumbs the depths of mystery. The chorus describes the mystery of life before reiterating once again, "We're better off for all that we let in." Images of everyday life blend with bigger symbols of power, control, and change. The middle verses take on the sources of power we so often take for granted, waxing hopeful that there will come a reversal of power:

> One day those toughies will be withered up and bent
> The father, son, the holy warriors and the president
> With glory days of put up dukes for all the world to see
> Beaten into submission in the name of the free

These lines offer an assurance that systems of power are only temporary and can be usurped for more righteous causes ("in the name of the free"), here illustrated with a play on Christian Trinitarian language. All this potential change is put into a perspective of our small beings when juxtaposed with the planetary movement that moves the universe forward. These overwhelming images contrast with the everyday image of one's personal relationships. The singer notices "crosses on the side of the road," evidence of tragic deaths, yet observed during something as

4. Saliers, *A Year a Month*.

ordinary as a daily commute; the scene prompts a feeling of gratitude in her.

The philosophical tone continues with grand observations made plain against life's ordinariness: "When I get home you're cooking supper on the stove / And the greatest gift of life is to know love." These final lines offer a profound insight into the struggle between hoping for grand gestures of change—the overturning of power structures—and the simplicity and importance of love. The song reflects a belief that it is necessary to have an awareness of the struggle and mortality intrinsic to our humanity, but it is equally important to fell grateful and find home in the warmth of love.

In 2010, the Indigo Girls released their first holiday album. Two of the songs included on *Holly Happy Days* rely explicitly on spiritual and religious images to further their prophetic imagination. Though they did not write "Peace Child,"[5] the lyrics and tone of the song fit in the larger theme of these final pages. The song is addressed to the Peace Child (a likely reference to the Christ child, given the context and season). The song is a meditation on the mystery of the Incarnation, illustrating the simultaneous chaos and beauty into which Jesus was born, or would be born, regardless of time or place:

> Peace Child,
> in the sleep of the night,
> in the dark before light
> you come,
> in the silence of stars,
> in the violence of wars––

5. "Peace Child" is a New Zealand traditional song, arranged by Emily's father Don Saliers for the album.

> Savior, your name.
> Peace Child,
> to the road and the storm,
> to the gun and the bomb
> you come,
> through the hate and the hurt,
> through the hunger and dirt—
> bearing a dream.

The words and music sing like a love song, though it is clearly theological, calling the child "Savior." Theological themes to do with the Incarnation permeate the lyrics; the child, the "savior" comes "in" and "to," and perhaps most significantly, "through." The final line in the second verse corresponds to the necessity of the imagination in speaking (and existing) prophetically. This child does not come in, to, or through all these things bearing a "sword," or to start a violent revolution, or even bear a "message"; rather the child comes "bearing a dream." The third and final verse reveals the substance and nature of the "dream" that is part of the coming of the Peace Child:

> Peace Child,
> to our dark and our sleep,
> to the conflict we reap,
> now come—
> be your dream born alive,
> held in hope, wrapped in love:
> God's true shalom.

The Peace Child's dream is rooted in hope and love; it is "God's true shalom," peace, justice, and freedom that is wholly spiritual and theological. This is not the peace of nations, but only the peace that can be called divine and has God as its source—the peace that passes all understanding.

A second song from their holiday album, "Your Holiday Song," is about peace and unity, belonging and healing.

The singers address children, encouraging them to "Gather 'round" and "make your joyful noise." The message of the song is about inclusivity, again stressing the persistent Indigo Girls' message of kinship and solidarity with the entire human family. The chorus stresses unity over diversity of religions, which seems to diminish the significance of differences, not in any effort to be syncretic or do away with differences, but to find ways to unite in spite of them. The final verse of the song explains why this is important and beneficial:

> For every voice lifted in song
> The sacred place we all belong
> A chance to heal a broken world
> with every voice in every song
> of every boy and every girl!

The message here is that sacredness permeates all the *forms* of religion whether it be "church bells," "silence," "goodwill," or "the feast after the fast." If we are able to work together and sing together regardless of our uniqueness we can unite in a vision of healing and unity. This song is consistent with the Indigo Girls' greater message of peace and unity. Amy and Emily are quick to insist on the sacredness of life and to resist the temptation to allow our *forms* (the fasting, or praying, or singing, or meditating) to divide us. Instead, these ought to be avenues of unity and healing.

The hope of the Christmas miracle, the promise of the Prince of Peace who came to bring "down the powerful from their thrones and [lift] up the lowly," and the fulfillment of the prophets of the One who "has filled the hungry with good things, and sent the rich away empty,"[6] is an apt note on which to conclude. Indeed, overt or not, it is this message that critiques injustice and hopes for justice

6. Luke 1:52–53.

for the whole world that is the core of the Indigo Girls' music. Moreover, their music does not remain complacent in the critique; through their songwriting they participate in prophetic proclamation—envisioning alternative ways of being, contributing to the collective imagination of contexts of equality, peace, and human freedom. Elsewhere, Emily has said, "my personal arc bends more towards hope and resurrection than complete despair."[7] The darker truth-telling in their music is not an invitation to despair, but rather the necessary journey through the realities of a broken world that must be acknowledged before one can right the wrongs and find the peace that passes all understanding, there is nothing more eternaly hopeful than that.

7. Saliers, *A Year a Month*.

Bibliography

Armstrong, Karen. *The Case for God.* 1st ed. New York: Knopf, 2009.

Begbie, Jeremy. *Resounding Truth: Christian Wisdom in the World of Music.* Grand Rapids: Baker Academic, 2007.

Bicknell, Jeanette. *Why Music Moves Us.* London: Palgrave Macmillan, 2009.

Brueggemann, Walter. *Hopeful Imagination: Prophetic Voices in Exile.* Philadelphia: Fortress, 1986.

————. *The Prophetic Imagination.* 2nd ed. Minneapolis: Fortress, 2001.

Carlile, Brandi. *Broken Horses: A Memoir.* New York: Crown, 2021.

Dyrness, William A. *Visual Faith: Art, Theology, and Worship in Dialogue.* Engaging Culture. Grand Rapids: Baker Academic, 2001.

Finch, Bill. "The True Story of Kudzu, the Vine That Never Truly Ate the South." *Smithsonian Magazine,* September 2015. https://www.smithsonianmag.com/science-nature/true-story-kudzu-vine-ate-south-180956325/.

Graham, Elaine. "What We Make of the World: The Turn to 'Culture' in Theology and the Study of Religion." In *Between Sacred and Profane: Researching Religion and Popular Culture,* edited by Gordon Lynch, 63–81. London: I. B. Tauris, 2007.

HeadCount. "Interview: Emily Saliers of Indigo Girls." September 7, 2016. https://www.headcount.org/music-and-activism/interview-emily-saliers-indigo-girls/.

Heschel, Abraham Joshua. *The Prophets.* 1st ed. New York: Harper & Row, 1962.

Honor the Earth. "About Us | Honor the Earth." http://www.honorearth.org/about-us.

Hubbard, Michael. "Interview: Indigo Girls." *MusicOMH*, March 2002. http://www.musicomh.com/music/features/indigo-girls-2.htm.

Indigo Girls. "1999: Come On Now Social Biography." http://www.indigogirls.com/correspondence/1999/bio.html.

———. "Activism." https://www.indigogirls.com/new-index.

———. "Biography—Despite Our Differences." http://indigogirls.com/biography.html. Accessed September 16, 2010.

———. "Correspondence: 2008-05-20: Election 2008." http://www.indigogirls.com/correspondence/2008/2008-05-20.html.

———. "Indigo Girls—The Rise of the Black Messiah—Behind the Scenes Ep. 3." https://www.youtube.com/watch?v=DUuRKu2zAF4.

———. "On Their 16th Studio Album." http://www.indigogirls.com/bio. Accessed August 31, 2022.

Jackson, Josh. "Indigo Girls on *The Paste Happiest Hour*." *Paste Magazine*. May 22, 2020. https://www.pastemagazine.com/music/happiest-hour/indigo-girls-livestream/. Video also available as "The Paste Happiest Hour: Indigo Girls." *YouTube*. https://www.youtube.com/watch?v=SJaLZc28O8M&t=2s.

Kincaid, Zach. "Indigo Girls Interview." *Matthews House,* September 29, 2009. http://www.matthewshouse.net/2009/09/indigo-girls-interviewl.html.

King, Martin Luther, Jr. "I Have a Dream." Delivered August 28, 1963. http://www.vlib.us/amdocs/texts/mlkdream.html.

Lambert, Susan, dir. *Indigo Girls: Watershed: 10 Years of Underground Video.* Sony Legacy, 1998.

Lilith Fair. "About Lilith Fair." http://www.lilithfair.com/content/about.

Masters, Jeffrey. "Amy Ray: Indigo Girls FOREVER(!!!)." Interview with Amy Ray. *LGBTQ&A,* March 30, 2021.

McClendon, James William. *Biography as Theology: How Life Stories Can Remake Today's Theology.* Nashville: Abingdon, 1974.

Migliore, Daniel L. *Faith Seeking Understanding: An Introduction to Christian Theology.* 2nd ed. Grand Rapids: Eerdmans, 2004.

Moltmann, Jürgen. *Theology of Hope: On the Ground and the Implications of a Christian Eschatology.* New York: Harper & Row, 1967.

———., *The Spirit of Life: A Universal Affirmation.* Minneapolis: Fortress, 1992.

Moss, Marissa. "An Interview with the Indigo Girls' Emily Saliers." *Huffington Post,* March 31, 2009. http://huffingtonpost.com/marissa-moss/an-interview-with-the-ind_b_180772.html.

Ragogna, Mike. "Brilliant Dreams: Conversations with the Indigo Girls and Sugarland's Kristian Bush." *Huffington Post,* July 29, 2010. http://www.huffingtonpost.com/mike-ragogna/embrilliant-dreamsem-conv_b_663241.html.

Ray, Amy. "2002-09-12: 'Queer and Fucked' in Response to 'Queer as Folk,' by David Hadju, *New York Times Magazine,* 8/18/02." http://www.indigogirls.com/correspondence/2002/2002-09-12-a.html.

———. "A Letter from Amy Ray April 8, 2003." http://www.indigogirls.com/correspondence/2003/2003-04-08.html.

———. "News from Amy May 29, 2009." http://www.indigogirls.com/correspondence/2009/2009-05-29-a.html.

———. "The Persistence of Optimism." Frank Gathering, University of Florida, March 3, 2017. https://www.youtube.com/watch?v=h6VYe6ATDp0.

Ray, Amy, and Emily Saliers. "Note from Emily and Amy March 24, 2009." http://www.indigogirls.com/correspondence/2009/2009-03-24-ea.html.

———. "Web Chat with Amy and Emily (Transcript)." http://www.indigogirls.com/correspondence/2002/2002–03–11–ae.html.

———. *A Year a Month* (blog). https://indigogirlsblog.tumblr.com. Accessed July 28, 2021.

Robertson, Jessica. "Rockin' Out Interview: Indigo Girls' Amy Ray." *Spinner.* June 11, 2007. http://www.spinner.com/2007/06/11/rockin-out-interview-indigo-girls-amy-ray/.

Sacks, Oliver. *Musicophilia: Tales of Music and the Brain.* Rev. and exp. ed. New York: Vintage, 2008.

Saliers, Don E., and Emily Saliers. *A Song to Sing, a Life to Live: Reflections on Music as Spiritual Practice.* 1st ed. The Practices of Faith Series. San Francisco: Jossey-Bass, 2005.

Saliers, Emily. "2000-12-19: Emily's Answers to Site Visitors Questions." http://www.indigogirls.com/correspondence/2000/2000-12-19-e.html.

———. "News from Emily 12.05.06." http://www.indigogirls.com/correspondence/2006/2006-12-05-e.html.

———. "Note from Emily June 16, 2010." http://www.indigogirls.com/correspondence/2010/2010-06-16-e.html.

Saliers, Emily, and Don Saliers. "Creativity Conversation." Conversation with Emory University Vice President Rosemary Magee. Emory University. September 24, 2010. https://www.youtube.com/watch?v=9PxThHyL2OI.

Sayers, Dorothy L. *The Mind of the Maker*. Westport, CT: Greenwood, 1941.

Schulz, Kathryn. "Let It Be Me: An Interview with the Indigo Girls' Emily Saliers." *Grist*, April 8, 2003. http://www.grist.org/article/let/.

Sölle, Dorothee. *Thinking About God: An Introduction to Theology*. London: SCM, 1990.

Tillich, Paul. *Dynamics of Faith*. New York: HapperCollins, 2001.

———. *Systematic Theology*. Vol. 1. Chicago: University of Chicago Press, 1951.

Tongson, Karen. "Karen Interviews Amy Ray of the Indigo Girls." Interview with Amy Ray. *Waiting to X-Hale*. Podcast Audio. July 10, 2020. https://waitingtoxhale.libsyn.com/website/karen-interviews-amy-ray-of-the-indigo-girls.

———. "Karen Interviews Emily Saliers of the Indigo Girls." Interview with Emily Saliers. *Waiting to X-Hale*. Podcast Audio. July 17, 2020. https://waitingtoxhale.libsyn.com/website/karen-interviews-emily-saliers-of-the-indigo-girls.

Tracy, David. *The Analogical Imagination: Christian Theology and the Culture of Pluralism*. New York: Crossroad, 1981.

Wainwright, Geoffrey. *Doxology: The Praise of God in Worship, Doctrine, and Life: A Systemactic Theology*. New York: University of Oxford Press, 1980.

Wiser, Carl. "Emily Saliers of the Indigo Girls." *Song Facts*. http://www.songfacts.com/blog/interviews/emily_saliers_of_indigo_girls/.

Wolf, Linda, Wind Hughes, McKenzie Nielson, and Sarah Lindsley. "INDIGO GIRLS: An Interview with Amy Ray and Emily Saliers." 2004. http://teentalkingcircles.org/8_interviews/indigoGirls.htm.

Wolterstorff, Nicholas. *Art in Action: Toward a Christian Aesthetic*. Grand Rapids: Eerdmans, 1980.

Woolf, Virginia, *A Room of One's Own*. Boston: Houghton Mifflin Harcourt, 1991.

Songs Referenced

"123," MP3 Audio, Track 5 on Indigo Girls, *Nomads Indians Saints*, Epic, 1990.

"Able to Sing," MP3 Audio, Track 12 on Indigo Girls, *Beauty Queen Sister*, Vanguard, 2011.

"All That We Let In," MP3 Audio, Track 5 on Indigo Girls, *All That We Let In,* Epic, 2004.

"Become You," MP3 Audio, Track 3 on Indigo Girls, *Become You,* Epic, 2002.

"Birthday Song," MP3 Audio, Track 8 on Indigo Girls, *Beauty Queen Sister,* Vanguard, 2011.

"Bitterroot," MP3 Audio, Track 8 on Indigo Girls, *Become You,* Epic, 2002.

"Cedar Tree," MP3 Audio, Track 13 on Indigo Girls, *Rites of Passage,* Epic, 1992.

"Change My Heart," MP3 Audio, Track 5 on Indigo Girls, *Look Long,* Rounder, 2020.

"Closer to FIne," MP3 Audio, Track 1 on Indigo Girls, *Indigo Girls,* Epic, 1989.

"Country Radio," MP3 Audio, Track 7 on Indigo Girls, *Look Long,* Rounder, 2020.

"Deconstruction," MP3 Audio, Track 2 on Indigo Girls, *Become You,* Epic, 2002.

"Everything in Its Own Time," MP3 Audio, Track 9 on Indigo Girls, *Shaming of the Sun,* Epic, 1997.

"Feed & Water the Horses," MP3 Audio, Track 9 on Indigo Girls, *Beauty Queen Sister,* Vanguard, 2011.

"Feel This Way Again," MP3 Audio, Track 9 on Indigo Girls, *Look Long,* Rounder, 2020.

"Free in You," MP3 Audio, Track 3 on Indigo Girls, *All That We Let In,* Epic, 2004.

"Go," MP3 Audio, Track 1 on Indigo Girls, *Come On Now Social,* Epic, 1999.

"Hammer and a Nail," MP3 Audio, Track 1 on Indigo Girls, *Nomads Indians Saints,* Epic, 1990.

"Hand Me Downs," MP3 Audio, Track 8 on Indigo Girls, *Nomads Indians Saints,* Epic, 1990.

"Hey Jesus," MP3 Audio, Track 5 on Indigo Girls, *Strange Fire,* Epic, 1987.

"History of Us," MP3 Audio, Track 10 on Indigo Girls, *Indigo Girls,* Epic, 1989.

"I Believe in Love," MP3 Audio, Track 3 on Indigo Girls, *Despite Our Differences,* Hollywood, 2006.

"John," MP3 Audio, Track 2 on Indigo Girls, *Beauty Queen Sister,* Vanguard, 2011.

"Land of Canaan," MP3 Audio, Track 10 on Indigo Girls, *Strange Fire,* Epic, 1987.

"Least Complicated," MP3 Audio, Track 2 on Indigo Girls, *Swamp Ophelia,* Epic, 1994.

"Leeds," MP3 Audio, Track 7 on Indigo Girls, *Shaming of the Sun,* Epic, 1997.

"Let It Be Me," MP3 Audio, Track 12 on Indigo Girls, *Rites of Passage,* Epic, 1992.

"Let it Ring," MP3 Audio, Track 10 on Amy Ray, *Prom,* Daemon, 2005.

"Look Long," MP3 Audio, Track 2 on Indigo Girls, *Look Long,* Rounder, 2020.

"Love of Our Lives," MP3 Audio, Track 3 on Indigo Girls, *Poseidon and the Bitter Bug,* Vanguard, 2009.

"Love's Recovery," MP3 Audio, Track 7 on Indigo Girls, *Indigo Girls,* Epic, 1989.

"Money Made You Mean," MP3 Audio, Track 8 on Indigo Girls, *Despite Our Differences,* Hollywood, 2006.

"Muster," MP3 Audio, Track 8 on Indigo Girls, *Look Long,* Rounder, 2020.

"Our Deliverance," MP3 Audio, Track 9 on Indigo Girls, *Become You,* Epic, 2002.

"Peace Child," MP3 Audio, Track 7 on Indigo Girls, *Holly Happy Days,* Vanguard, 2010.

"Pendulum Swinger," MP3 Audio, Track 1 on Indigo Girls, *Despite Our Differences,* Hollywood, 2006.

"Perfect World," MP3 Audio, Track 4 on Indigo Girls, *All That We Let In,* Epic, 2004.

"Philosophy of Loss," MP3 Audio, hidden track on Indigo Girls, *Come On Now Social,* Epic, 1999.

"Power of Two," MP3 Audio, Track 5 on Indigo Girls, *Swamp Ophelia,* Epic, 1994.

"Prince of Darkness," MP3 Audio, Track 4 on Indigo Girls, *Indigo Girls,* Epic, 1989.

"Rise of the Black Messiah," MP3 Audio, Track 10 on Indigo Girls, *One Lost Day,* Vanguard, 2015.

"Rock n Roll Heaven's Gate," featuring P!nk, MP3 Audio, Track 6 on Indigo Girls, *Despite Our Differences,* Hollywood, 2006.

"Salty South," MP3 Audio, Track 15 on Indigo Girls, *Poseidon and the Bitter Bug, Deluxe Version,* Vanguard, 2009.

"Scooter Boys," MP3 Audio, Track 8 on Indigo Girls, *Shaming of the Sun,* Epic, 1997.

"Shame On You," MP3 Audio, Track 1 on Indigo Girls, *Shaming of the Sun,* Epic, 1997.

"She's Saving Me," MP3 Audio, Track 11 on Indigo Girls, *Become You,* Epic, 2002.

"Shit Kickin'," MP3 Audio, Track 1 on Indigo Girls, *Look Long,* Rounder, 2020.

"Sorrow and Joy," MP3 Audio, Track 11 on Indigo Girls, *Look Long,* Rounder, 2020.

"Southland in the Spring," MP3 Audio, Track 4 on Indigo Girls, *Nomads Indians Saints,* Epic, 1990.

"Tether," MP3 Audio, Track 6 on Indigo Girls, *All That We Let In,* Epic, 2004.

"There's Still My Joy," MP3 Audio, Track 12 on Indigo Girls, *Holly Happy Days,* Vanguard, 2010.

"They Won't Have Me," MP3 Audio, Track 12 on Indigo Girls, *Despite Our Differences,* Hollywood, 2006.

"Trouble," MP3 Audio, Track 4 on Indigo Girls, *Come On Now Social,* Epic, 1999.

"Virginia Woolf," MP3 Audio, Track 8 on Indigo Girls, *Rites of Passage,* Epic, 1992.

"War Rugs," MP3 Audio, Track 5 on Indigo Girls, *Beauty Queen Sister,* Vanguard, 2011.

"Watershed," MP3 Audio, Track 7 on Indigo Girls, *Nomads Indians Saints,* Epic, 1990.

"We Get to Feel it All," MP3 Audio, Track 4 on Indigo Girls, *Beauty Queen Sister,* Vanguard, 2011.

"When we Were Writers," MP3 Audio, Track 4 on Indigo Girls, *Look Long,* Rounder, 2020.

"Wood Song," MP3 Audio, Track 7 on Indigo Girls, *Swamp Ophelia,* Epic, 1994.

"World Falls," MP3 Audio, Track 3 on Indigo Girls, *Nomads Indians Saints,* Epic, 1990.

"Your Holiday Song," MP3 Audio, Track 4 on Indigo Girls, *Holly Happy Days,* Vanguard, 2010.